Darlene 5/2016 (handwritten)

Positive Thinking
Will Never Change Your Life...
But This Book Will!

8 chapters (handwritten)

The Myth of Positive Thinking
The Reality of Success

All that limits us is our belief that "such things" are impossible (handwritten)

DAVID ESSEL

Believe in + everything if you think that "you" on... belief (handwritten)

Motivation, perseverance, self-believe (handwritten)

ISBN-13: 978-1523395859
ISBN-10: 1523395850

WHAT PEOPLE ARE SAYING ABOUT THIS BOOK...

"David Essel boldly flings open a hidden door of wisdom—a different perspective on the 'positive' that is the keystone to living our greatest self. He captivates us with stories and straight talk, elegantly clear, filled with profound knowledge derived from his own experiences and insight gleaned from thousands of interviews with luminaries at the pinnacle of success. David's authenticity is impeccable, his insight is brilliant, and his style is irresistible."

Dianne Collins, Creator of QuantumThink® and 6-time Award Winning Author of the Bestseller: Do You QuantumThink? New Thinking That Will Rock Your World

"David asks us to put our attention on the importance of faith (love) over fear. Through action steps, not just our thoughts, we are able to sit with our discomfort without fear in order to learn and grow from the experience. This gives meaning to our suffering and allows us to help others. By choosing love we effectively walk through the fire, not around it, and in doing so empower ourselves to limitless heights."

Scarlett Lewis, Author, Nurturing Healing Love: A Mother's Journey of Hope and Forgiveness

"David nails it in this book! A great read to re-train your thinking habits and achieve your goals!"

Tracie Cyganiak, Bikini Fitness Competitor

"In his new ground breaking book, "Positive Thinking Will Never Change Your Life..." David has made the connection between simply having a positive belief to moving into positive action. Everyone who follows his advice in these pages will finally find the success they are looking for. Go."

Joe Cirulli, CEO, Owner, Gainesville Health and Fitness Centers

"I always say, "My dreams inspire my direction, but my footsteps take me there." David Essel has done a great job of outlining exactly what it takes to make your dreams come true in his new book, "Positive Thinking Will Never Change Your Life...... But This Book Will!"

Natalie Pace, Best Selling Author, "The ABC's of Money"

"David's new book is going to finally help wake this world up to what it REALLY takes to create lasting success in any area of your life. Enough of the "intentions, affirmations and wishes for success!" In these pages you will find the path to the life you truly desire. "Positive Thinking will NEVER Change Your Life..." will become the new "bible" for success. ACT on those principles today."

Ray Higdon, Millionaire Author, "Vibrational Money Immersion"

"My hope is that the billions of people that read this book are touched in a powerful way, realizing that the only real "secret" to positive personal growth and success is in the commitment, work, daily writing and repetition David so expertly details and outlines as his recipe for success!"

Terrance Essel, President, Owner, Superior Fax & Laser and The Toner Kings

"I enrolled in one of David's seminars crafted from his powerful book, " Positive Thinking Will Never Change Your Life....But This Book Will!" with my three boys and the end result was impactful beyond my wildest imagination. By incorporating David's techniques we all gave our dreams wings!

John Biffar, International Filmmaker

"This book isn't really about not thinking positively. It's about under-standing what actually constitutes positive thinking. It's about being free to examine your thoughts, feelings and beliefs, accepting yourself and others, and facing your own inner and outer truth, as an action step to-ward positive change. That doesn't always produce the warm fuzzies that we generally associate with being positive, especially in the beginning of the process of self discovery. David's book, comes as a bit of shock ther-apy that can help us awaken out of denial, get real and understand that the way out is through if we want to create miracles in our life."

Rev. Renee Bledsoe, Founder, Addiction Alchemy & Church of Spiritual Light

DEDICATION

I dedicate this book to Wayne Dyer, who positively influenced millions of people around the world through his teachings and simply with his presence while he was here on earth with us.

After my first interview with Wayne in the early 90s, he expressed how much he enjoyed spending time with me, discussing the principles of helping people to become more successful in life. I'll never forget what happened next. He asked how he could help me push my message forward into the world.

I couldn't believe what I was hearing! Here was one of the top authors of our day, even back in the early 90s, taking a few moments to ask me how he could help me. I didn't have an answer then, but after our next interview about six months later, I asked if he would mind writing an endorsement of what he felt our program brought to the world.

Within a few minutes, he had recorded a spot for my national radio show and told us we could use his endorsement anywhere we wanted to. He said simply this: "David Essel's mission is to help you to become more alive in every area of your life."

What a beautiful statement from one of the greatest teachers of our time. This is one of the many reasons why I am dedicating this book, a book whose premise is all about positive change, to Wayne Dyer—my friend, mentor, and more. May he rest in peace.

ACKNOWLEDGEMENTS

I've never met an author who ever said they wrote a book by themselves. It's always a team effort. I want to thank Renée Bledsoe and Raven Dodd, for their expertise in the technical, editorial and artistic layout of the book. They were both phenomenal to work with. I would like to thank Christine Dupre for cover design collaboration.

Of course, I am deeply grateful to all the contributing writers, whose experience, expertise and philosophies are so in sync with my own. I love each and every one of them for taking the time to share their expertise with us in this book. You can find out more about each of them in the index at the back of the book.

I want to acknowledge my mom and dad, who I am blessed to still have with me on earth, as well as my brother, Terry and my sister Marydiane. They are always so supportive in every endeavor I take on. I love them for that.

And I want to thank YOU! The searcher. The dreamer. The person who is looking to change not only their lives, but the lives of those around them. I salute you, I praise you, and I thank you for supporting me over the years with all of the different projects we've unleashed!

Love,

David

TABLE OF CONTENTS

Forward by Eldon Taylor, Ph.D.

Introduction: Shattering the Illusion of the Positive Thinking Movement

FORWARD

Your reality is largely a matter of perception, but we all interpret almost everything somewhat differently from one another. However, it is our perception that defines much of our lives and our perception is based largely on our beliefs.

Research has repeatedly demonstrated just how easy it is to manipulate a person based on their expectation. This is turn shapes their perception, and is an outgrowth of their life beliefs. Perception can therefore lead one to make mistakes and/or to find success. Take for example the idea that rich people do not deserve their wealth. They should spread it around. We should all share and share alike. This is a common belief today in many circles and one we hear repeated even in our politics. As I write this forward, I am reminded that there is a current front runner seeking the office of President of the United States who is openly in favor of wealth redistribution and declares himself to be a socialist. Just assume for a moment that you are one who feels this way and yet you have decided to become an entrepreneur and create your own business. Do you not see the dissonance here?

When your perception of wealth is something akin to, 'it is the root of all-evil,' or "it is easier for a camel to go through the eye of a needle than for someone who is rich to enter the kingdom of God," then you have sentenced yourself to failure when it comes to building financial prosperity. When your perception recognizes that money is not evil, but rather the wrong use of it that is to be avoided, then there is nothing to stop you from becoming super successful! With money your wealth can be used to help others by providing jobs, contributing productivity to our world, and aiding the less fortunate.

Positive thinking can therefore be very powerful, for it can mold an expectation that leads to innovative perception and ultimately success at whatever you are undertaking. That said, as you will discover in David's new book, it isn't positive thinking that gets in your way. No, rather it's the failure to take the initiative and act!

Unfortunately a common belief today arises from a bestselling book that promises fortune if you but only magnetize your thoughts with what you want. You might expect it to be a best seller when you think about it, for it basically tells us we don't need to work hard for anything—we can just visualize it. Let me flesh that out a little. The so-called "Secret" suggests that our thinking is like a giant magnet that attracts kind, and thus the over used and immature notion that there is this thing called the law of attraction that is thought based alone. Thank God that's not so, or many of us might have experienced some truly unpleasant results from our passing moments of fatigue, frustration, anger and the like! Still, there are those adamant believers of this nonsense who insist that everything that happens to us is brought to us because we have "magnetized" it with our thoughts.

This is so ridiculous that I once even heard a popular guru of the law of attraction state that another teacher of the law of attraction, one who had organized a sweat lodge that led to the deaths of two followers, had attracted this because of his thinking. How can any intelligent and sensible human being look at a victim of rape, incest, or any other violent crime; and/or the cancer or terminal patient, and insist that they attracted their situation due to their magnetic thoughts?

As you read David's bold new work you will discover exactly why this is not only nonsense, but also very dangerous nonsense at that! David is a positive thinker who has empowered the lives of many through his teachings. In this book he explains how important your expectation, perception and life beliefs are. He will share with you in the pages that follow just how you can actualize your ambitions. This powerful book urges action and renounces the idea that success can simply be magnetized using incense, a vision board, affirmations and so forth.

We live in a world of action. We know time only as a result of action. Before this there was that, and after this there will be—and on and on it goes. This book is all about action—the action it takes to realize your personal best in everything you do. With that come the rewards you are seeking, whatever they might be. You will learn how to succeed whether it's fame and fortune or love and joy. Enjoy the journey and here's to your very best in everything you do!

Eldon Taylor, Ph.D., FAPA
NY Times Bestselling Author of "Choices and Illusions"

"There is no coming to consciousness without pain.
People will do anything, no matter how absurd,
to avoid facing their own Soul. One does not
become enlightened by imagining figures of light,
but by making the darkness conscious."
– C.G. Jung

INTRODUCTION

Shattering the Illusion of the Positive Thinking Movement
(How This Book Was Born)

It probably comes as a shock to many people who know me, or have listened to our national radio show for 24 years, or viewed our television segments, that I'm writing a book to shatter the illusion of the positive thinking movement. But it's true. Someone had to do it, and the response has been out of this world! People have been waiting for an individual to take a stand against the somewhat insane way we've been attempting to teach people how to change their lives.

Several months ago, I was contemplating writing my next book. We had finished eight, and I knew another topic was ready to be birthed, but I wasn't sure what it was. We have many outlines already on file, ready to be written, but I knew there was something different bursting within. An awareness inside was gnawing at me to take a chance and create something that could be controversial, but at the same time highly effective in helping people to radically change their lives

So I called my good friend Renée Bledsoe, the editor of several of my books, and I shared this idea with her. What if I wrote a book to dismantle the illusion around positive thinking? What if I actually proved to people that what we've been taught in regards to how to change our lives is not true, and on one level, is an absolute lie? I hesitated and waited for her response. Renée is one of those people that will never tell you what you want to hear, she only says what she believes is the truth. We've known each other for almost 40 years, and she's never let me down. That doesn't mean she's always agreed with me, but she's never let me down in regards to being honest with her thoughts. Her response was instantaneous, and it surprised me.

"Sweetie, you are on to something big! You need to do it right now! I think the timing is excellent, as people are looking for more direction on this."

I was thrilled. I was over the top thrilled. Even if Renée had said to me that it's the worst idea in the world, I would've written the book anyway. But with her endorsement, coming from an editor that I totally respect, I was now ready to go.

As I started to create the outline, another idea slowly crept into my head. One morning I woke up and said, "Wait! I can't be the only one that thinks this way." I thought of all the people that I've interviewed over the years who are best-selling authors, experts and more; I knew they must feel the same way. Even though no one had come out and said it in the way that I wanted to, I knew they must agree.

So with that, the project began to go in a slightly new direction. I've never collaborated with other authors before, and I didn't need anyone to write chapters, but I needed their personal stories—real personal stories. At one point they may have believed in positive thinking and still do to this day, but they had to do something radically more than that to create the success they wanted. Here's a copy of the letter that I drafted and sent to those whom I wanted to be a part of this book. These were people I fully respected and loved. Many of these people I had interviewed multiple times on my national radio show. In this letter, I wanted them to see my vision and join with me if they agreed 100% with my desire to dispute the myth of the power of positive thinking.

Dear _____,

I'm in the process of completing my ninth book and would love to see if you would have any interest in giving me a paragraph or two from your perspective ... if you agree with the premise that I'm going to present. As you probably know, my work in the world of personal growth began 30 years ago in the world of health and fitness, and then transferred into the world of sports psychology. In 1990, 25 years ago, I then started working with what I refer to as the "general population" ... anyone who needs any help, in any area of their life.

From loving relationships, to addiction recovery, to career changes, attitudinal changes, financial freedom, overcoming emotional, physical or sexual abuse ... there is not an area of life that we haven't been fully immersed in during this period of time. But something dramatic has happened along the way, which is the premise of our new book. We believe that our society has been hoodwinked into accepting certain psychological and personal growth dogma that is almost entirely false in its ability to deliver the amazing end results it promises.

I know we're going against the sacred holdings of many people ... and we're going to rock the boat. But we're not going to rock the boat just for the hell of it, we're going to rock the boat to give people hope that once again they can live the life of their dreams. The topic I'm referring to is that of positive thinking, and how too many people are taking it at its most simplistic nature in the hopes that it will change their life. It simply won't. The title of my new book is the following: Positive Thinking Will Never Change your Life ... But This Book Will! The Myth behind Positive Thinking, The Reality of Success.

I think too many people have fed our population a bill of goods that does not deliver. Think this way ... and you'll achieve what you desire. Make this vision board ... and become a million-aire. State affirmations with a certain tonality, and you will attract your life partner. Does this stuff ever work? Absolutely! If it's a miracle.... But how often do miracles like this happen in the average person's life? Well, if we look at the number of books sold, which promise us that all we have to do is think a different way or feel a different way ... you would think it's happening every day!

What I have found in 24 years of interviewing on my national radio show, the most outrageously successful people in regards to money, their bodies, love, or attitude ... is that not one of them has ever claimed that positive thinking brought into their lives, the incredible success they've achieved! No, not one! I don't care if we're talking about Deepak Chopra, the late Wayne Dyer, Meatloaf, Kenny Loggins, from homeless to millionaire Joe Cirulli, Dr. Joe Dispenza, Dr. Joe Vitale, Suze Orman ... or T. Harv Eker ... or Marianne Williamson ... or Mark Victor Hansen.... Not one of these individuals ever said to me that because they created a vision board or thought positively every day, or wrote affirmations of abundance; not one of them ever said this is all they did to create incredible success.

In the book I'm proposing, we will talk about the power of positive thinking to elicit short-term change, but that the real key, the reality of success, has much more to do with what we do, who we hang out with and our willingness to get uncomfortable on a daily basis. I would love to feature a short few paragraphs of your experience, if you agree with my philosophy. You might give a story about how your life changed in regards to your health, finances, relationship, body, or business through incredible effort, as well as the correct thought. I will be sharing from my life, actual miracles to prove that yes—sometimes positive thinking alone—on a very rare basis, can radically change our lives! Because I don't want to take that hope away. But we will also be explaining that about 98% of the time, my clients who achieved radical changes, did so by stretching themselves out of their comfort zone on a daily basis. They did this by getting mentors or hiring professionals that would push them to the edges of what they thought was possible in order to create great abundance, freedom from addiction, long-term weight loss, or an amazing love relationship. I highly respect you and your work, and I would love to have you as a part of this book.

If you would please respond and let me know if you would be willing to do this, I will get back to you, and we can pick a date in which you could have your material sent to me. Again, I'm only looking for several paragraphs ... maybe a personal experience of yours that says positive thinking is wonderful, but this is what I had to do to really change my life. I know this book is going to re-vive hope in the human race! I know when people see that they can't just sit and look at a vision board, or state affirmations to change their lives ... that something else must be added, they will be inspired to take action!

They know it cannot be this simple, but they desire it to be! We want to get them out of the discouragement of life and into a system that actually will help them achieve their dreams.

I am 1000% committed to this program as I want to be a catalyst of change in this world, not a charlatan selling programs to get people to think they can sit and get rich—or sit and lose weight. Won't you please join me? Won't you help me to get the re-ality of success out there, so we have more people in this world ac-tually becoming successful instead of just looking at others and wishing? This is the time for all of us to come together, to help

boost self-confidence and self-esteem in our world.and at the same
time help people see that they are worth what they desire.
Sending you all my love,
David Essel

The response was instantaneous. Eldon Taylor, one of the most respected experts in the world of the subliminal and subconscious mind, responded in less than 24 hours.

"I'm on board, David."

Next I contacted JJ Virgin, best-selling author in the world of health and nutrition; followed by Dianne Gray, Executive Director of the Elisabeth Kubler Ross Foundation; and Dianne Collins, author of the best-selling book, *Do You Quantum Think?* The list goes on, including my personal mentor, Joe Cirulli, who has so much integrity and knows what it's like to be down and out as he went from homeless to multimillionaire. You're going to read the stories of many individuals who will inspire you to shatter your own illusions around the power of positive thinking and do what needs to be done to create everything you've always wanted.

I'm excited that you're on board for the ride. I'm excited to share with you concepts that could challenge you, that might make you feel uncomfortable, that might make you say, "Why haven't I thought like this before?" That's the purpose of this book; to challenge you, question you, and then finally give you a pathway to success. You deserve everything you desire, and I will help you get there.

Chapter 1
Why Positive Thinking Will Never Change Your Life

So, why is a guy who loves positive thinking, and has worked in the positive thinking, personal growth industry for over 30 years, now writing a book to dismantle the myth of the power of positive thinking? The truth is that I love positive thinking. I'm one of the most positive people you will ever meet. If you ask my brother, and he's totally unbiased of course, he will tell you that he's never met a person that has gone through more adversity and maintained such a high-powered positive attitude—than me. But I did not get or stay positive strictly by thinking only positive thoughts and saying or writing affirmations. I became and remain positive by relentlessly facing my own shadow and seeking the truth, not simply covering it with positive affirmations. Accepting and coming to terms with the truth, the good, the bad and the ugly, is what lead me to the actions that helped me change my life for the better.

As I witnessed so many clients who were disappointed and disillusioned after following the advice of best-selling books on using the power of the mind to change their life, and not seeing any real and lasting changes, I realized that positive thinking alone had some serious limitations. As I saw that the coaching work that we offer naturally addresses the need to jump off the positive thinking bandwagon, and take positivity to the next level by guiding our clients into taking powerful and positive action steps necessary for deep and permanent change, I knew that I needed to share this with everyone.

The people that find their way to our work are only a tiny percentage, compared to the millions upon millions of people who have invested time, money and effort into weekend seminars, CD courses, DVD programs, and books, that have been telling us for years that if you think a certain way, you can attract the perfect soul mate. Or if you build the right type of vision board, you can become a millionaire. It's all a bunch of crap. And this book will prove that not only are these theories and philosophies unfounded in reality, but that they could actually be hurting more people than they help.

I don't believe for a second that other authors, teachers or speakers, have done this intentionally. I really think everyone has good intentions in this industry, at least for the most part, to help people create the life they want. But positive thinking alone just doesn't work. Unless of course, a miracle takes place—which it could—I'm all for miracles, but usually people that achieve any type of significant success do it by something much greater than positive thinking alone.

Let me give you an example of a client that came into my office a number of years ago in the same dejected state of mind that I've seen in so many people. She had followed a very popular book that recommended she write positive affirmations about what she wanted in her life for 45 minutes every day. She walked into the office with piles upon piles of journals, 45 minutes of writing affirmations every day for two years. She never missed one day of writing! And yet here she was, almost broke, having not been in a healthy relationship for years, struggling with self-confidence and self-esteem. Everything that she was told she would accomplish by writing these affirmations had never come true. I was her last stop. There was nothing else left that she could think of doing other than investing some of the little money she had in savings, into my coaching program.

Within eight weeks, we were seeing a dramatic turnaround in her attitude. Twelve months later she was rocketing to the top of her profession, making more money than she's ever made, doing exactly what she's here on earth to do. So what was the difference between the work that we did together and the program she was following by a best-selling author that has sold millions of books? The answer you will find later in this book. You'll find that taking specific steps on a daily basis is the key to great success with your financial situation, your body, your attitude, your relationships, your spiritual path or anything else that you want to accomplish in life. She was proof positive, that by only using positive thinking, nothing changes in our lives. Now there are exceptions. Miracles happen. I'll never take that away from anyone. But instead of sitting around and waiting for miracles to happen, we will teach you a formula, which will help you create the success you've always wanted. And I'm so excited to share it.

Another client came to me, searching for her soul mate. She had gone to a soul mate weekend workshop, had read several bestselling books on soul mates, and all of them said to do the same thing; write down a list of the attributes that you want in a partner, look at that list every morning, close your eyes and see that person coming into your life. That's all. That's all she needed to do. She attended several weekend intensives on finding your soul mate, and all the experts said to do the same thing, as well. She knew it must be a fool proof program with all these experts agreeing on the "remedy", which consisted of affirming and visualizing the end result of her goal.

But after a year and a half of following the systems and not getting any closer to love, she decided to give our program a shot. She had heard from another friend of hers that what we did was very unique, and it helped her friend create success in life. As we went through her goals and I started sharing some of our work, she looked at me with the most skeptical face I've ever seen in my life. I almost started laughing. I didn't, of course, but she was shaking her head saying, "I don't think this is going to work, David."

As she shared with me that he would be six foot two, blonde hair, blue eyes, making $150,000 or more per year, loves to travel, and loves to lavish his girlfriend with gifts, I told her that this whole thing about writing the physical characteristics of the man of her dreams, was an awful lot of fun, but it was not the way to go. I told her instead to go home and write out the personality traits she was looking for, the personal interests that she was hoping her soul mate would have, and the traits a healthy partner would bring, like integrity and honesty, etc. And, as importantly, to create a list of "deal killers in love", characteristics of a man that would absolutely not work for her. Now, she was even more skeptical than when we first started talking. She went home, did exactly what I said, and came back in.

She threw the list in front of me and said, "This is boring!"

She was not excited at all to start thinking about visualizing some guy who was honest, funny, filled with integrity, and a really great communicator. Boring. Boring. Boring.

I told her to follow the program just to amuse me and that she needed to get out of her normal routine in order to meet this person. For example, go to lunch with a guy and have fun, even if you know he's not your perfect match. I told her that you never know what can happen by going out with someone you're not instantly attracted to. He might just have a roommate, a brother or a cousin that is a perfect fit for you. She said, "OK," rolled her eyes with that skeptical look and walked out the door.

A short while later I heard from her, and she said that she wasn't going to finish her last session, that she had gotten everything she could out of my program. Even though her previous program with the best-selling soul mate authors never worked, she thought that it was probably a better path for her. I never heard from her again—until four years later.

I was speaking at a major conference on creating the life of your dreams, and after my presentation there was a long line of people waiting to ask me individual questions. As I moved through the line, I came to the very end and there was someone that I recognized, but I couldn't remember from where.

We started small talk and then she said to me, "I don't know if you'll remember me David, but I was a client of yours about four years ago, and I was looking for a partner."

Automatically I said, "Oh my Lord, it's the soul mate lady!"

We both laughed hysterically, and then she invited me for coffee. She told me she had a very interesting story I might want to listen to.

As we sat down, she started telling me how skeptical she had been about my program. No big surprise there right? But then she said after several months of going back to her old ways of looking for "the perfect guy" who was six foot two, blonde hair, $150,000 salary or more, once again wasn't getting her anywhere. So just for the hell of it, she pulled out the homework that she and I had worked on and decided to go after it full force. She told several girlfriends that she was looking for a guy that was funny, who could make her laugh daily, that was filled with integrity, and about all the work that she and I did on personality characteristics. At first several of them were skeptical as they asked what about the six foot two, blonde haired knock out that she'd always been talking about and visualizing? She laughed and told them that that was the old version of herself, but the new one was going to try something different.

A few weeks after telling her girlfriends about her change of heart, a former male coworker contacted her and asked her to start getting together for lunch simply to brainstorm business ideas. She was in a great state of mind because she wanted to grow her business, and so she said yes. They ended up meeting every couple of weeks for lunch and it was simply business—nothing more than that. Until one day when her business accountability partner got up to use the restroom, one of her girlfriends who happened to be in the restaurant at the same time came over.

"Oh my gosh, who is the new guy? You guys are electric together! You're laughing constantly; tell me who he is."

My former client laughed and said, "You've got to be kidding me, that's just John. He's a former coworker and we're getting together simply to inspire each other to become more successful in business. I have no interest in him other than that."

As her girlfriend walked away, she said, "Honey, I'd rethink that. I haven't seen the sparks fly between two people the way they do between you and your so-called business accountability partner, in a long time. I think there might be something more there than you even know."

As her friend walked away my former client let out a big sigh and said, "You've got to be kidding me. John is short, bald, not in great shape, and he doesn't fit any of my characteristics."

But over the next couple of weeks she kept pulling out the list that she and I had created that had nothing to do with physical appearance or money. And she started to see that John had everything on her list that she was looking for. He did make her laugh constantly. She loved the way he listened to her intently and gave her more individual attention than any man she'd ever met. She was shocked to be thinking that this could be a soul mate.

As she continued the story, there were tears in my eyes because I knew in that moment, what was about to happen.

"David," she said, "we've been married for three years. He is the most amazing man I've ever met in my life. And I found him not through positive thinking or visualization; I found him by being grounded in the actions that you gave me. Thank you so much. I am truly indebted to you and to the work you do, and I've told several girlfriends that they need to quit the nonsense and get in touch with you if they want to find a program that actually works in manifesting their desires."

There are thousands of clients' stories that I could share that ended up the same way. They are people from all walks of life who are ready to see their life change, but have no idea how to do it other than the bestselling books that tell them to think, or visualize their desires. It doesn't work. Throughout this book you'll read more stories of people just like this. And on top of that I have hand-picked a selection of New York Times bestselling authors who have created the life of their dreams through the marriage of positive thinking and visualization—and more importantly—the necessary action steps.

You'll read the stories of people like Joe Cirulli, who went from homeless to multimillionaire; Eldon Taylor, New York Times bestselling author, who is possibly the top expert in the field of the subconscious mind and subliminal thinking; financial expert, Natalie Pace; incredible Arielle Ford, a guru among gurus in the world of soul mates; Dianne Collins, one of the top experts in quantum thinking; Dianne Gray, Executive Director for the Elisabeth Kubler Ross Foundation; JJ Virgin, New York Times bestselling author who has an amazing story about applying action steps and saving the life of her son.; and Scarlett Lewis whose powerful story moved a nation.

And there are many more stories you'll read throughout this book, on top of those mentioned, that prove once and for all that positive thinking alone will never change your life. I am well aware that I'm taking a huge risk here in my own industry, of alienating some of the top experts in the world when they read what you're about to read right now. I'm willing to be a leader and a myth buster. I'm willing to take that chance for people like you, who truly deserve and desire a different life, but have been told part of the truth—not the whole story. You will get the whole story here, to manifest what it is you've always wanted into your life.

I still read some of the most positive thinking books ever written, and I reread the ones that truly have immense value, like *Think and Grow Rich*, by Napoleon Hill, one of my favorite books that I've probably read front to back 10 to 15 times! And did you know, that in this book, Napoleon Hill never says that you can think and grow rich? Isn't that amazing! He never, ever says that. In every success story in his book, people found a way to think positively, but they had to do something much more to create the life they created. Or what about Wallace Wattles, the author of the best-selling book, *The Science of Getting Rich*? Throughout the book he talks about faith and positive thinking, but he also says unequivocally, those will never be enough!

You will also find that I'm a huge fan of using positive affirmations on a daily basis! I also love visualizing my end result on a daily basis. My morning starts out with intense rituals based on prayer, meditation, affirmation and visualizations. I've been doing this for over 30 years now. My personal work in the world of positive thinking began when I was a kid, with huge dreams to be a National Basketball Association All-Star. I had pictures of Earl "The Pearl" Monroe, Jerry West, Mike Newlin and many other NBA stars all over the room in my house. I would see the pictures of these All-Stars, and imagine myself playing in the NBA.

I practiced 365 days a year in Syracuse, New York, which means shooting over snow drifts, in pelting rain, and calling myself Jerry West and Earl "The Pearl" Monroe as I spun around imaginary defenders and scored the winning basket in the NBA finals! I've been a longtime fan of both affirmations and visualizations, but hard work would eventually lead me to a position on the Syracuse University junior varsity Division One basketball team. It took years of dedication as I mentioned, and my parents scrounging for money to send me to basketball camp after basketball camp. And what I'm going to be proving throughout this book is that you can have what you want, but you have to be willing to do things differently than you have up to this point in your life.

So when you read about the books that say to affirm your way to the perfect body, or to create a vision board and see yourself with a home in Fiji or Bali and making $10 million a year, don't throw the books away; read them and enjoy them. But don't count on them to have a very big effect on the end result of your goals. We believe that the power of thought and visualization is crucial to success, however, I'm going to take a big risk here and say it's about 20% of your success. That's it. That's all. Think positively all you want, but if you don't do the rest baby, you're not going to get the life that you want.

I remember living in a beach house on Siesta Key, Florida, and literally on the walls in every room I was writing affirmations. I am a multimillionaire. I am sober. I'm competing in my first bodybuilding competition. I will tell you that for as long as I lived there none of that came true. I never made $1 million. I never got sober while living in that house. And I surely never competed in a bodybuilding competition, even though I was in great shape compared to the average individual. The key point I want to stress throughout this book, is that positive thinking is wonderful, but it will never change our lives! I wanted to believe that these bestselling authors knew something I didn't. And that if I surrounded every visual space on my walls with positive affirmations, surely something had to change. It didn't. It never will. And I had to learn this the hard way.

After about two years of repeating this practice, I knew something had to change. That something was me. There had to be something in my daily action steps, or more specifically my lack of daily action steps that would bring me closer to making $1 million, getting sober, having the body that I've always wanted. I knew there had to be a way, I just hadn't found it yet. But I also knew from my own experience, and that of thousands of clients, that it really had nothing to do with thinking in a different way, or visualizing in a different way.

As you will read later on, I trained with some of the most amazing minds in this industry. In the world of visualization, I interviewed Denis Waitley, Brian Tracy, and Kelly Howell, yet no matter how many different visualization techniques I used, I never achieved the end results I wanted! Until one day I started living differently. OK, I'm getting ahead of myself. You'll find out throughout the rest of this book what everyone needs to know. The steps are simple, powerful, proactive, and they will give you the life you want.

For 24 years I hosted a nationally syndicated radio show. We began with Westwood One back in 1990, transferred over to XM satellite radio, and then went to iHeartRadio. In 24 years of interviewing the top experts in the world of personal growth like Deepak Chopra, Wayne Dyer, Suze Orman, Dr. Joe Dispenza, Dr. Joe Vitale and celebrities like Kenny Loggins and Meatloaf; athletes like Roman Gabriel, the great quarterback; and Keith Mitchell, the All-Pro linebacker; not one of them ever talked about achieving huge success in life by thinking a certain way. Not one. Don't you think that if it was possible to think or visualize our way to success, that at least one person in 24 years would have told me that is all it took for them to achieve success?

You must agree with me. There would have to be at least one person over the years that would have said to me, "David, this is all I did. I got up in the morning. Read some affirmations. Stared at my vision board. And it just happened. The most amazing woman in the world came to deliver my pizza, and then the Publishing Clearinghouse people came and gave me $25 million dollars, and somehow, David, I'm not sure how this happened, within seven days I was competing in the International Bodybuilding Competition, and I won!"

As I write this, I'm laughing. I hope you're laughing, too. I truly believe that you can accomplish just about anything you desire. Almost anything. And I know it's the same for me. I've gone from making very little money to a lot of money. I've gone from having a decent body to a fantastic body. I've gone from not trusting women to creating some of the most beautiful relationships I could ever imagine. I say these things to tell you that there is a way that will work for you and for anyone. And the best-selling authors and experts, and successful people you will read about are backing me 100 percent. It's time to bust the myth of positive thinking once and for all. It's time to rock. Let's go!

Chapter Summary

Slow down for just a moment and answer the following questions so that you may get the most out of this life changing book:

1. What was covered in detail in this chapter?

....

....

....

....

2. Of the topic, or different topics covered, which point was of most interest to you and why?

....

....

....

....

3. What is one action step you can take this week, that is relevant to this topic, that will propel you to create the life you desire?

....

....

....

....

Chapter 2
What is Positive Thinking?
The Benefits and Limitations of Thinking Positively

Over the years there have been one million definitions of what it means to be a positive thinker or what positive thinking really is. Of course, we could say it's looking at the bright side of life, knowing there's a solution to every problem. Gratitude, on a daily basis, is a form of positive thinking that we will talk more about later on in the book. Looking at the glass as always full; that would be the ultimate in the world of positive thinking. Byron Katie introduced us to a side of positive thinking when she released her work, *Loving What Is*. This means that no matter what is going on in life, we embrace it. The benefit of this is that we can see the goodness in everything, the great things that have happened, as well as the challenges. That could just be the ultimate in positive thinking.

After my interview with the president of HeartMath Institute, Howard Martin, it became evident through all of the research they've done that when people think positively, there's actually a cascade of chemicals released in the brain within seconds of doing certain types of heart centered breathing and positive thinking techniques. Amazing! Can you imagine that you have this much control? One of the benefits of positive thinking would be to release a cascade of positive chemicals in the brain, such as serotonin, dopamine, GABA and more!

Along the same lines, during one of my several interviews with New York Times bestselling author, Gregg Braden, he shared with me how people from an indigenous tribe in South America were able to use this heart centered breathing and thinking as a way to deal with severe setbacks in their lives. Forced to move from the jungle habitat that was their natural environment for centuries, these individuals were now living in mountainous regions, totally out of their element. Their way of living had to change. Their way of farming had to change. And yet as Gregg interviewed these people, he found that they held no resentment whatsoever. They naturally were living in a heart centered way. Quite simply, they were accepting what is. Adapting to change: positive thinking turned into positive living. And there was little stress among these people. Think about you and me. We are in traffic today, and it slows down, and our heart rate increases, frustration occurs, all because of traffic. That is actually the opposite of someone living in the world of positive thinking and action, in the world of adaptation.

Through science, we know that the benefits for people who think positively on a daily basis would be an increased function of the immune system and a decrease in diseases like the common cold. Many people who make dramatic changes in their attitude will see a decrease in the effect of migraine headaches, chronic fatigue syndrome, fibromyalgia, and many other emotionally-based disease conditions of the mind and body. Positive thinking works; it's amazing.

Did I just say that? Did the author of a book saying positive thinking will never change your life on its own just say that positive thinking is ... Amazing? Absolutely! I love it. I use it daily, throughout the day, in the afternoon, in the evening; there will not be a time of the day when I'm not taking advantage of the incredible benefits of positive thinking.

Positive thinking will also deepen our friendships, partnerships, marriages, and relationships with family, children, neighbors and more. Positive thinking will help us deal with financial stress, and it may even lead to an increase in our income, especially when we're competing in the marketplace where people are looking for someone who is confident and empowered. We all need to take advantage of the power of positive thinking more often. When used correctly, positive thinking can turn the struggles of life into thriving, not just surviving. One of the most powerful examples of this has to be from best-selling author, Victor Frankel. His New York Times bestselling book, *Man's Search for Meaning,* depicts the terrible challenges he faced in the concentration camps in Germany, and his ability to take that struggle and turn it into something meaningful. Powerful.

Here's a man who lost his family and many friends in the concentration camps, was himself, living under torturous conditions, on the verge of dying from malnutrition and yet he found his purpose in life. He found, in the middle of this horrendous situation, that his purpose and truly everyone's purposes is to serve others. Can you imagine that? As we complain about our wife, husband, boyfriend or girlfriend, children, and coworkers, a man imprisoned in a concentration camp in Nazi Germany found his purpose for living. But wait—he didn't just find it—he actually applied it in the middle of the most stressful experience anyone can imagine. Positive thinking became positive doing.

This is taking positive thinking to the highest level of awakening. This is the profound effect that positive thinking can have not only on an individual's life, but on the lives of those around us.

Yet, while this all sounds great, there is a dark side to the world of positive thinking. There's a yin to every yang in life. And one of the purposes of this book, is to break the myth of positive thinking, and look at the darkness that happens when we put our head in the sand and pretend that our life can be changed through thought alone. Or worse yet that our life is actually fine right now when it absolutely is not.

Positive thinking can give false hope to the individual who's caught up in the insanity of so many of the philosophies that are being promoted today. Think positively and change your life? I think not. Unless it's a miracle. This false hope is something that can actually hold people back instead of propelling them forward. Repeating the affirmation … I am a millionaire … when you're earning $20,000 a year is absolute crap. It gives a person a sense of false hope without any chance at all of changing their current situation if they don't move way beyond positive thinking.

Positive thinking in this form can be used as an example of escapism. Instead of looking at reality, we might flood our brain, at least temporarily, with these feel-good chemicals, but we're living in illusion. It's not reality. It's a form of escapism that can actually hurt us. If we're faced with a serious medical condition or other situation we may pretend they're not there. We will repeat affirmations saying how we are healed by universal light, or universal energy, or God. And while it might work sometimes, the odds are not in our favor. This form of denial of reality, has led to the demise of many marriages, incredible financial stress, suicide, and premature death due to the denial of the disease state that is occurring within the body.

Before you shake your head and throw this book out the window, let's look at the truth I just stated. I'm not saying that we shouldn't think positively and use positive affirmations and visualization to heal the body when we're in the middle of disease, or to help us turn our finances or our marriage around. The problem is that so many programs are trying to teach us that this is all we have to do. And it's nonsense. Hogwash. We need to wake up to shatter the illusion of positive thinking, so that we can all achieve what we really desire in life. It is possible. But we must be willing to look reality in the face.

I am a perfect example of this. For 30 years I've been teaching this whole concept of positive thinking, positive action and personal growth. I started in the world of health and fitness, then moved into sports psychology before I started to bring these messages to the general population. That means we work with just about anyone, with any challenge, and one of the tools we use is positive thinking. However I took it a little too far for a very long time and struggled in an area of life I could have easily healed years ago.

For over 20 years I would wake up every morning, and repeat this powerful affirmation. "I'm a child of God, happy, healthy and sober today." What a beautiful affirmation. What a beautiful, powerful statement to say first thing in the morning, noon and night, as I did every day. So what's the problem? By 8 o'clock every night after my last client was done, I would open the first bottle of wine. Depending on the day, how much stress I had, the difficulty of helping clients work their way through some real challenges in life, it could go to a bottle and a half or two bottles easily. And I justified it. I was living in complete denial, even after helping hundreds upon hundreds of other people during this period of time to get sober, I was justifying and rationalizing my alcohol usage every night.

And this positive affirmation actually helped me to stay in denial. Can you see that? Here I'm repeating every day that I'm a child of God, healthy, happy and sober, which allowed me to stay in complete denial. Yet, by 8 o'clock at night I was back at the bottle. Why? I deserved it. I worked hard. Successful men drink. We relax through glass after glass of wine, bourbon, vodka, valium, food, marijuana, prescription drugs, street drugs… television, radio, "workaholism". You get the picture?

But as long as we're thinking positively in the morning, noon and early evening, the addictions can continue. Positive thinking used incorrectly can actually support our denial, helping us to keep our head in the sand about harmful behavioral patterns, such as shopping, sex or any addictions we refuse to fully face. You name it; it's possible to think positively, stay in denial, and hold back our own personal or professional growth.

One of the greatest guests that I've had on my national radio show several times over the years is Dianne Collins, author of the best-selling book, *Do You Quantum Think?* She is absolutely brilliant and talented. She takes the topics of quantum thinking, quantum doing, quantum theories and makes them understandable to the masses. She's amazing, and she has a great way to differentiate the power of positive thinking from wishful thinking or hopeful thinking. This is Dianne's story; sit back, grab your herbal tea and enjoy!

DIANNE COLLINS – QUANTUM THINKING

"All of life evolves. We progress to higher understandings over time, and this book contains a key message in evolving our awareness in the realm of the very important field of personal growth. I don't think any person or leader in the personal development field intentionally led people astray in focusing on the power of positive thinking. It is simply that we were lacking knowledge of the finer distinctions of the role of mind and thinking in creating results and manifesting our passions and dreams.

In my own work I make a vital distinction between "positive think-ing" and QuantumThinking. While it's always good to have posi-tive thoughts, QuantumThinking is not the same as positive think-ing in that positive thinking is typically a "positive affirmation" attempting to cover over a negative belief you are holding as "the truth." When you QuantumThink you recognize this. You have ac-curate knowledge of the creative dynamics of mind, what I like to call "the physics of mind." You realize 3 key quantum discoveries: reality is not static; reality is context-dependent; and reality is multi-dimensional.

What this means is that you and I can shift and shape our results and our destiny. That we are not stuck with even our most intensely held "beliefs." That just because you have a thought doesn't make it "the truth." That what happens is determined by the context we choose to live from. It means you are thinking multi-dimensionally —knowing that the physical, energetic, mental and spiritual as-pects of your goal must be attended to if you want to master how to manifest them.

Years ago I created – in thought – the intent that I am a masterful communicator and popular media personality. It wasn't "the truth" at that time, or even a "belief." It was a context I chose. I didn't create the intent and then sit back and rely on the fantasy of wishful thinking to have it happen. I took action. I studied the genre. I threw myself in front of audiences even when I felt scared.

I watched and listened to thousands of shows with the intent to learn the finer distinctions of the art of being a masterful communicator—a media personality who enlightens, entertains and engages people so they are moved into productive, inspired action. I hired a publicist and was interviewed on more than 400 hundred radio and TV shows, Internet webcasts, and podcasts. I am still and will always be learning and looking for opportunities to go to my next octave of mastery and success.

Mind is a creative substance. Thought is powerful indeed. Everything ever invented by humankind began with a thought. Intent expressed as thought is not a cause and effect dynamic. It is a field dynamic. Many results will occur that are consistent with your intent. Action is required. Strategic thinking is necessary. Immersing yourself in the field of your desired profession or art form is wise. Hiring a coach with your desired expertise is brilliant. You develop in a co-creative dance with thought, opportunity, action and follow-through.

The results you attract may be business opportunities. Results may show up as new people in your life. Results could be a lightning bolt idea you hadn't thought of before or even dreamed possible! Intent has the power to generate all of that. However, the possibilities you generate with your intent require engagement on your part. Intent requires intelligent, wise engagement.

Intent is like planting a seed. You plant the seed, you nourish it with light and water and nutrients, and you allow it to take root and become a sapling, grow and flourish. You interact with the unfolding. Intent expressed as thought is like this. You allow for the energy-intelligent mind field connections to be made – and you step in and take action as you become aware of the opportunities."

Look at what an expert in thought power just said! Over 400 action packed interviews have opened the doors to her amazing success. I love it.

I remember working with a client that came to me with many challenges. She was 30 pounds overweight, she used alcohol in the morning to get her day started and would plan daily business meetings around lunchtime or happy hour so that she could have a couple more drinks just to stay in control, calm and happy. Her marriage was average at best. She struggled with her children. Her career was stagnant and boring, and while she was busy as could be, it was not fulfilling at all. In other words, when we're in that situation, we're living with our heads in the sand. And she was a positive thinker! She would read positive books, listen to positive CDs, but there was no action to get her out of the unhappy state she was in.

As we worked together, the very first thing we found was that there were huge resentments against her mother and father that occurred during a very difficult childhood. She went through amazing challenges as a young girl, and was put in charge of raising brothers and sisters when she was barely old enough to take care of herself. The resentments were huge. Even though she had done a lot of work in the world of media, and was extremely attractive, she had very low self-confidence and self-esteem. That's not unusual. Couple that with trying to stay positive, and talking to people about the power of positive thinking, which she did, and she could have stayed stuck for many more years.

We worked together for over a year. After the first year of working together, she went through our life coach certification training program to become a Certified Master Life Coach. Her life was on fire. Not only did she become a more positive thinker, but the key here was that she became an extreme positive doer. She faced her fears. She got out of denial. She looked in the mirror, and for the first time saw someone she could admit she didn't like. Through all of her hard work and effort she lost 30 pounds, dropped alcohol; her marriage went through the roof in the most positive ways; she rebounded and reconnected with her children, and she left a career that was less than fulfilling to begin her own business. What a turnaround! If she had tried to rely on doing this on her own, simply by thinking positively, none of that would have ever happened.

Are you starting to get the picture? Are you starting to see that we must dismantle the old beliefs around positive thinking and create a new reality? Dianne Collins put it perfectly as she made the separation between positive thinking and quantum thinking. Today is a day you can make this decision for yourself. We have so much more to share throughout this book, more experts and more success stories to bring you to a higher level of awakening, and success.

Another profound radio guest from my show is Dianne Gray, the Executive Director of the Elisabeth Kubler Ross Foundation, and President of Health Hospice Communications, Inc. Dianne faced such a deep tragedy in the loss of her young son and learned the importance of going into grief, through grief, instead of trying to dance around it with positive thinking. I am in awe of Dianne and her work. I am in awe of her as a human being, and the powerful message that she shares through her work.

Here is Dianne's story about how she moved into and through grief after the loss of her young boy. Take a big breath. Slow down. As you read, understand that you can't cover up grief by thinking positively. You can't avoid it by being busy—or drinking—or eating. Dianne is here to teach us a valuable lesson. While we all want to think more positively, we've got to get out of the illusion that positive thinking is the answer to life's challenges.

DIANNE GRAY – FACING GRIEF HEAD ON

"In 2005, my beloved 14 year old son died following a decade long struggle with a one-in-a-million neurodegenerative disorder. Like many who have observed long term suffering or endured the loss of a loved one, my world was turned completely upside down and trying to find a new identity that didn't include having my son at the end of my fingertips, seemed an insurmountable task.

The smallest things left me in a puddle of tears— a song, a movie, a scent. I found the silence in my home deafening while conversely, loud sounds and rooms filled with laughing people left me disoriented and trying to find my emotional center. I was raw, emotionally, physically, spiritually. I felt I would never, ever have the ability to walk as I had before— upright with confidence and most importantly, in peace.

The first three years of my grief are a blur now— thank goodness...because I'm sure it wasn't very pretty, though I had a full library of self-help books on my nightstand. Many of them abided by the clinical models for healing grief while others eschewed the practice of healing grief by "staying positive" as though that alone would flip the switch in my confused brain and mangled heart. Incredibly however, most did not cut to the chase. They did not explain simply that the grief process can be ugly, but in large part, there is only one way to heal; by going through, not around, your pain.

Furthermore, most content I read did not discuss that in large part, the grief process involves making choices — lots and lots of choices. Some need to be made repetitively, like the decision to eat healthily, exercise often, drink lots of water, avoid overindulgence in any one thing. Other choices however, required nerves of steel, facing fears while leaning full on into whatever made me cringe (or sob) the most... like watching the "first day of school" school bus pull away without my son or shopping for the family Christmas tree alone.

By facing head on into what I perceived to be the most painful event of the moment, I found that no matter what, the emotional pain of loss did not physically kill me. In fact, I found the converse to be true: that I was much stronger than I imagined possible and that acknowledging my pain and in fact, sitting deep in it for a bit, it allowed me the ability to pull myself up.

But ignoring one's emotional pain— by telling oneself to simply "stay positive" therefore implying that the grief/loss can be healed by surrounding oneself with the latest practice in positive psychology is a dangerous practice indeed...because it does not validate the very thing we know to be true: that someone we love died and the pain is at times, searing.

Healing grief takes time— sometimes years in fact and it can only occur when we are honest with ourselves and those around us — that in grieving those who have died, we are also acknowledging how very much we still love and sometimes ache for, their physical presence. In the end though, love lasts and relationships continue —of this I am sure."

Hold on to Dianne's words, "Ignoring one's emotional pain by telling oneself to simply stay positive is a dangerous practice" indeed. Positive thinking alone does not work in life.

We've gone over the benefits of positive thinking and there are many! We've gone over the limitations of positive thinking, and there are even more limitations when positive thinking is used incorrectly than there are benefits. We proved it in this chapter. Yes, think positively every day. I want to repeat this. I wake up every day and the first 45 minutes to an hour is all based on gratitude, positive thinking, visualization, prayers for this world and prayers for people who don't like me, and of course, prayers for people that do like me. I pray for everyone. I want you to do the same, I want you to get into the mindset of using positive thinking, heart centered breathing, and heart centered thinking every day. But face your fears. Face your insecurities. Face your struggles head on. Ask for help from someone outside of you to shatter the illusion of positive thinking, to get out of denial, to get out of justification, and move into the existence that you want.

Positive thinking is amazing—but it alone will never change your life.

Chapter Summary

Slow down for just a moment and answer the following questions so that you may get the most out of this life changing book:

1. What was covered in detail in this chapter?

....

....

....

....

2. Of the topic, or different topics covered, which point was of most interest to you and why?

....

....

....

....

3. What is one action step you can take this week, that is relevant to this topic, that will propel you to create the life you desire?

....

....

....

....

Chapter 3

Positive Thinking versus Beliefs: Beliefs Will Always Win

For centuries now we've heard statements that we want to be true, such as, "If you want something bad enough, if you believe you can have it, you can achieve it." It sounds great, and we all want it to be our reality. But unfortunately it's not; it's actually filled with tons of illusion, misconception, and denial of the reality of life. It's not enough just to believe, or to want something with all your heart. There has to be something much more than that in order to create the life you want.

And how can I be so sure that the statement about "whatever you believe, you can achieve" is erroneous? From the simple fact that if it were true, every person that ever attended a personal growth seminar, or read a personal growth book and believed really hard that they could become a millionaire, would all be millionaires. If they truly believed they could be a size two or size six, they would have already done it. If all it took was a positive statement, in order to attract your soul mate or the perfect house or the perfect career, everyone who has ever been involved in the world of personal growth would have everything that they want right now. It would be that simple. As you can see, maybe even looking at your own life, it's not that easy.

No matter how hard I want to believe in one of the greatest dreams I've ever had, it will never become my reality. I want so bad to be a starting guard on the Miami Heat basketball team, right next to Dwayne Wade. I want to average 25+ points per game and bring them to another championship. No matter how many positive affirmations I say, no matter how deep my beliefs might be that I am worthy of playing with the Miami Heat, no matter how desperately I want it, it will never happen. Now there may be millions of other things that I can want, that I don't have right now that I can achieve, but this is one that will never be my reality.

Not everyone can become a size two or four. No matter how hard you believe it to be true it's not going to happen with your belief systems only. Not everyone will become millionaires; no matter how many seminars you go to that say anyone who wants to become a millionaire could become one by believing a certain way, it's just not true. And you know what I'm saying is factual. So it takes a heck of a lot more than believing something to achieve it. Once again this is the premise for this book. It's the whole reason I'm writing it. We've got to get out of the nonsensical belief system that if you believe or think about something, you can achieve it. Please, let's toss this crap out and get to the truth.

For 25 years I've had clients that I've worked with from all over the world, including, the United States, Spain, Mexico, Canada, Sweden, Australia and New Zealand. So many of them come to me with the same story. They've attended these breakthrough weekend intensives. They've attended one day, seven day and fourteen day intensives, to shatter beliefs and to create the dream world they've always wanted. But the funniest thing is, it doesn't work. In most cases, attending the three day seminar or seven day seminar or twenty-one day seminars is not going to change your life! Let me repeat this, all these seminars are great and fun, but they will not change your life!

It takes a hell of a lot more than 21 days of attending someone's resort in some foreign country, or right down the street from you, in order to change internal belief systems that you may have held since your were 2, 10 or 18 years of age. It's a lot more complicated than that. But here's a tip. If you're going to spend money on an intensive workshop, make sure you have enough money to hire a coach for the next 50 weeks. I'm being dead serious here. If you don't have an accountability partner to carry on after the wonderful exciting dynamic weekend workshops, nothing will change long-term. I will say that about 75% of people I work with have been to some type of intensive, hoping that the investment of a certain amount of dollars and their time will help them to radically change. Every once in a while someone might change in a big way through one of these intensives. But for the most part we don't. We need a hell of a lot more work, effort, dedication, and accountability before life is going to radically change. So do yourself a favor. If you're going to put money into these workshops, and I love them as well, just make sure you're putting money into an accountability program for the 10 or 11 months after that program is done. Now that is where you'll see lasting change.

So what are beliefs? A belief is an internal expectation of something you perceive to be real or true. I remember being raised in a democratic household, and while my parents have changed their opinions in some ways over the years, when I was a little kid, Democrats were good and Republicans were bad. It was pretty simple. It always seemed that my parents voted for the Democrat in the presidential race. And even though I'm not that interested in politics, until I left my house at 18, I pretty much believed the Democrats knew what was best for our country. Now it doesn't have to be factual to be a belief system. A belief is just something that we hold as true.

In our life coach certification courses we teach a simple definition for a belief: a belief is simply your reality. It's that simple. Whether the belief is healthy, unhealthy, true or false, it really doesn't matter. Once you have a belief about anything in life, it becomes your reality. Beliefs are incredibly powerful.

And where does a belief come from? Most of our beliefs in life are formulated between the ages of 1 and 18. This includes everything from beliefs about relationships, money, career, and education, to alcohol, vacations, and God. Most of our beliefs come from the core family environment. Many of our beliefs are so deep in our subconscious reality that we don't even know we hold them. We may try to convince the world that we love ourselves while we're 20, 50 or 100 pounds overweight, or as we smoke and drink regularly; or eat sugar on a nightly basis. But, the internal beliefs might be saying a totally different thing. This is why changing belief systems is much more complicated than a three day workshop.

Beliefs can also come from intimate relationships. If a woman has been hurt multiple times by men, she may believe all men are dogs. If a man has been taken to the bank by a woman, some men will believe that all women want is their money. We may have a belief system regarding sex that is based on religion. Sex is only for procreation. During sex, you don't ask for what you want. That's not being a nice man, or that's being a naughty girl.

Beliefs can come from reading a bestselling book that says, "Imagine checks coming in the mail and they will." Or, "Affirm daily that you are in excellent health, and at your ideal body weight, and it will come true." Ridiculous beliefs like these have been accepted by so many people because they read it in a bestselling book. So sad. So true.

Beliefs can come from college fraternities, from our first job, from our first mentor or first boss. They can come from elementary, middle and high school or college coaches, teachers or music instructors. The list goes on and on.

I remember struggling as a kid in school. I was more athletic than I was academically inclined. I had a breakthrough in third grade and I can still remember it. I was a terrible speller. Even though my mom and dad spent time with me to become an adequate speller, I just couldn't grasp it. Then, in elementary school, Sister Vedette at Saint Rose of Lima School, took me under her wing. She was strict. She was strong, but I could tell she really cared. In third grade everything changed. My belief that I wasn't smart academically shifted, all because one nun showed me she cared. Now she didn't show me she cared by letting me get away with things, but by using discipline, and a voice that said she believed in me.

After that experience I had greater confidence. It wasn't that my grades were always wonderful, but I knew I could do certain things academically that I didn't think I could do before. Athletics still ruled my life, and I still had dreams of playing in the NBA through elementary and high school.

Later on in life, I had this very intense experience, which proved I was as creative as I wanted to be. I remember a friend of mine came over to my house, when I lived on Siesta Key, Florida. She was sitting on the couch, while I went to take a shower. I came out of the shower only to see her crying hysterically as she was flipping through a pile of papers. As I looked down, I was absolutely shocked! Somehow she had found my diary, my daily diary that was filled with all kinds of pain, addiction, doubt, frustration, and being hurt in love.

As she looked up at me with tears streaming down her face, she said, "David, this needs to be a book. This is not just your story; this is everyone's story."

I had never imagined that I was creative enough to be an author. Yet, in that moment, one friend's special words shattered the beliefs that I was not a creative person. I became a published author. That first book, *Phoenix Soul: One Man's Search for Love and Inner Peace*, opened up a whole new world of internal creativity that I never really knew existed. But remember, I had completed a year of writing, 365 days of written action steps that she was reading. Action changes beliefs. What you're reading right now is my ninth book, and I continue to be amazed at how beliefs from the past can either hold us back, or be shattered and propel us forward. I want this book to help you shatter any limiting beliefs and propel you into the life you want. But it's going to take a lot of work, at least at first.

So here's a question for you. How do you know that the beliefs you currently hold about any area of life are true? Or how do you know that they're absolutely false, created by a conscious mind that wants you to believe that you're worthy of deep love, an amazing body, all the money you could ever want, a wonderful relationship with your higher power, being on task with your life purpose, and maybe most importantly, being fully in love with yourself?

Here's the shocking answer to that question. If you truly believe that you are deserving of making $50,000 or $100,000 or $1,000,000 a year, and you hold that truth as an affirmation that you learned through a book or seminar, and you repeated it on a daily basis; you should be seeing progress towards that goal every year if the belief is grounded in reality. If someone were to say to you, are you really worthy of making $100,000 a year? You would stand staunchly in your power and answer, "You bet I am. I am worthy of $100,000 a year." Whether that belief is truly yours or an illusion, can only be seen by answering this question: "How close are you to making $100,000, not just this year, but for the past 10 years?" This is one of the ways that we dismantle illusion and look at the reality of what our beliefs are. Just because you spout won-

derful affirmations, it doesn't mean those are your true internal beliefs at all.

Let's use the same example with your body. Many people,
after doing a weekend workshop or reading positive books, will
come up with affirmations that sound something like this: "I am
loving my body and I'm a strong and healthy size 8," They may say
that for years. But if you want to know what your beliefs really are
about being worthy of a size 8 body, or size 2, or size 16 or whatever your goal is, look at the size of your body for the last 10
years. Are you slowly moving down from a size 18 if you started at
size 18 ten years ago? Are you getting much closer now to the size
6, or size 8, or whatever size you claim you believe you're worthy
of? If you're not, then the belief that you're worthy of being a size
2 or 8 is an absolute false belief. It's just not true. No matter how
many statements you want to make looking in the mirror that you
are worthy of something that you don't have, if you have not been
strongly progressing towards that goal for the last 10 years, then
that is not your actual belief at all.

If you were to ask most people on the street, do you really
love yourself? The answer would be, "Oh, yes! I love myself entirely." Now, you just might. Maybe you're one of the people that
really truly does love yourself. But if you have addictions of any
kind: money, sex, food, alcohol, nicotine … then that's not a sign
of self-love at all. Now if in the last 10 years you decreased all of
your addictions, and you have one more left to handle, then you
could say, "Yes, I'm on the path of self-love."

If you return regularly to unhealthy friendships or unhealthy love relationships, and that has been your pattern for the last 10 years, then to believe—"I truly love myself"—would not be accurate. Do you see where I'm going here? If you struggle with codependency and put everyone else's needs first, because it feels right, you could be a martyr. When your life is deteriorating while everyone else is being taken care of, that would not be a sign of self-love. So what we need to do is look at the reality of our life to see what the reality of our beliefs are. Enough of this Pollyanna thinking—enough of these false beliefs. Let's do something now, through this book, to change your life forever.

Positive thinking can release a cascade of chemicals, as I mentioned earlier, that make us feel good in the moment. Repeating affirmations that make us believe we love ourselves, or are worthy of millions of dollars, or a great love relationship, could actually cover up the reality of the fact that we don't love ourselves, or that we don't feel worthy of more money. If positive thinking is used incorrectly, you are creating false beliefs, which will actually derail you from any measurable movement toward success in life.

In order to understand beliefs a little further, we've got to get into the conscious and subconscious mind. I've mentioned throughout this book that over the years, the people I've interviewed have been absolute experts in the power of the subconscious mind. Eldon Taylor's story is coming up in just a little bit in this chapter. Gregg Braden, New York Times bestselling author; Joe Dispenza and Michael Kiefer are all experts in the world of the conscious and subconscious mind. I've learned so much from these guests on my radio and TV shows. And then of course, books by individuals like Maxwell Maltz and Joseph Murphy have opened my mind to the power of our conscious and subconscious mind. Let's take a look at both.

Our definitions of the conscious and subconscious minds have been created over 30 years from all the work that we've done in the world of positive growth. These are not textbook definitions. If you Google them on the Internet you might find something different. But just as we explain the conscious and subconscious mind in the way I'm going to right now, we have literally helped thousands of people, through our coaching programs, reach great freedom and success in their lives. And it's because we have truly understood how both of these parts of the mind work.

The conscious mind is analytical and logical. It is the part of the mind that says, "I think it's a good idea to get up at 7 AM tomorrow so I have time to meditate and pray before I go to work." The conscious mind is the one that goes to the workshop and writes down all the goals you want to accomplish. The conscious mind hires the coach to help you break through and become financially successful, or lose weight, find a new job, create the deepest love in your life or recover from an affair. That's the role of the conscious mind. When used correctly, the conscious mind is outrageously powerful.

The conscious mind is the part of the mind that says, "Let's say affirmations tomorrow morning, let's visualize, let's pray, let's get to the gym, let's eat really clean, let's forgive my partner from the past who stole from me because forgiving her or him will actually free me. Let's forgive my partner from the past who cheated on me, not to let them off the hook, but to allow me to be free of any resentment so I can be powerful and in alignment with my current life path." These are the workings of the conscious mind.

The subconscious mind is quite different. Here's something interesting that many people don't know. The subconscious mind says, "I want comfort; I want to stay in the known." The subconscious mind doesn't differentiate between healthy or unhealthy in regards to comfort zones. For the alcoholic, drinking every night is a comfort zone, and the subconscious mind will defend any thoughts from the outside world that says we have a problem. The subconscious mind will say, "I deserve it. This is the way I relax. I'm only going to have a couple."

The subconscious mind will come up with all kinds of rationalizations and justifications to get you to buy that shirt on sale or to eat that sugar at night or have just one more cigarette. Or, to use prescription drugs, because after all, the doctor said they were OK. The subconscious mind is only concerned with you doing what you're doing right now. Now let's look at this exciting thought. If you are a millionaire, if you have 10 percent body fat right now, if your work serves humanity, if you are free of all addictions, your conscious mind and your subconscious mind are in 100% alignment! Congratulations! That's where we all want to be.

But if you're not there, this tells you that you are not aligned on the conscious and subconscious level. This is where it gets tricky.

Let me repeat the statement. The subconscious mind is basically in control. And all it cares about is the known. It does not want you to get out of your comfort zone, even if your comfort zone is getting up at eight o'clock to rush to be at work by nine and to create all kinds of stress. The subconscious mind will justify every flaw in the world to tell you that it's better to stay up until midnight to enjoy yourself and to relax with four hours of mind numbing television, then it is to get to bed at 10 PM and get up at 6 AM and have a relaxing morning. Does this all makes sense? Some of the subconscious/conscious mind stuff can be really confusing. At one level, the subconscious mind is ingrained in comfort zones that are not healthy. It's not your ally. It's not your best friend! Anyone who tried to quit overspending or drinking or smoking or over eating, knows the statement is true. The subconscious mind has held us back from making any radical changes.

"You don't have the money right now to spend on rehab. Saks Fifth Avenue only has this sale one time a year. I could go to the gym tonight, but it would look really good if I was at the bar with all the other sales people."

The subconscious mind does not want you to change. But once you turn it around, it will radically accept change on a regular basis. Fascinating isn't it? So here we have this part of the mind justifying all these crap behaviors and belief systems, but when you turn it around you will never go back to your old way of living or thinking about money, food or love. You will be a radically changed person, which is what this book is all about.

This concept is a big part of our Life Coach Certification programs. Every time we talk about the conscious and subconscious mind, someone raises their hand and says, "David, why is it so hard to change the subconscious mind?"

Imagine this. Your belief systems about money, how to handle stress, love, etc., were formed between the ages of 1 and 18. Let's say you saw dysfunctional love: if your dad or mom were always at work to avoid intimacy, if there was abuse of alcohol to avoid intimacy, if there was passive aggressive behavior in love. If people never spoke their feelings because they were codependent and didn't want to rock the boat, then your mind from the age of 1 to 18 had been programmed to see that these unhealthy forms of love were actually normal! So as you grow up, you simply repeat that which you locked in to your sponge like subconscious mind between the ages of 1 and 18. This is why it's so hard to change these beliefs that have been held for so long.

There are two processes that go on in the subconscious mind and the conscious mind that either propel us forward or hold us back. The number one thing that holds us back is something that we have termed human nature. Human nature has been with us from birth. And the simple definition is, "human nature equals our desire to get the most out of life through minimal effort". And this happens from the day you were born. Unless they are raised in an extremely toxic, addictive or abusive environment, most babies' needs are met instantaneously. You cry a certain way and you get fed. You cry another way and your diaper gets changed. You make a "googly" face, and everyone freaks out and says you're the most adorable baby in the world. So human nature, our desire to get the most out of life with minimal effort, is fed to the highest level possible while you're a baby moving through infancy. But wait a second, a huge shock is about to happen.

As most psychologists will share, potty training is one of the greatest disruptive events that happens in a young person's life. Instead of strolling down the mall with mom and dad and just going to the bathroom anytime you want to in your diapers, all of a sudden there are new rules. You have to get out of the stroller, or off your bike and come into the house and use a what? A toilet? What the heck is that for? I just want to go in my pants! But we're no longer going to be able to do that. Human nature is starting to become shattered. Our desire to get the most out of life with minimal effort is coming to an end.

Next we have to clean up our room. Then there's homework. Then there are chores. Everything is starting to interfere with the way we want to live our lives and we are not happy campers. But even as adults, we still have the desire to get the most out of life with minimal effort, until we change the subconscious mind. Lottery tickets are still selling off the charts; many people with very little extra money, spend it on lottery tickets every week hoping to make it big. To hit it rich. Infomercials on TV that say you can have thinner thighs in 30 days with this piece of equipment, which will cost you $29.95 a month for 24 months, are tapping into human nature. Urging us to get the most out of life with minimal effort. Millions upon millions of dollars are being wasted by people looking to fulfill that internal drive of human nature. We want instant gratification.

Again, these thoughts of human nature, wanting the most out of life with minimal effort are being drilled in to the subconscious mind from a young age. And most of us don't have the body. money, relationship, or career that we want, and we are still living at this level. We're trying to find shortcuts in life. We're trying to find the easy way out. And advertisers and marketers tap into your human nature to get you to buy the car, home or ring that you can't afford. Books like *The Secret* do the same thing; as they say that we can basically do nothing other than affirm and visualize success in order to create the life of our dreams. It taps into "our desire to get the most out of life with minimal effort." It will never work.

I still have to battle my own human nature. I remember buying extra properties that I could not afford during the housing boom in Florida. Why? Because I wanted to flip them and make money or hold onto them for two years and make a killing. It's called greed. It's also called human nature. I wanted the most out of life with minimal effort. If someone told me I could buy this property and in six months sell it and make $100,000, I was all in. Great. Human nature. Do you see what I'm saying? Even though I teach this stuff, I got sucked into the same thing that so many other people did. And I lost it; yes I lost my investments because of human nature and simple greed. If it sounds too good to be true, dammit—it probably is! Let's wake up together.

The antidote we are teaching in our courses on human nature is called human success. Human success is defined as anything that will bring a huge benefit to our life, which will demand a huge effort to create change. Human success says that we must do the uncomfortable; we must be held accountable on a daily basis. In order to change the subconscious mind set, we must be willing to commit 365 days in a row to doing that which we would rather not do, in order to see the change we want. In order to shatter the belief that we need alcohol or sugar, or we absolutely need the 40th pair of jeans that are on sale, we will have to release our own human nature.

When I met Eldon Taylor on my nationally syndicated radio show, I'd known of his work for a number of years. This guy is amazing. I believe by far that he is, without a doubt, one of the preeminent minds in the world of personal growth. His specialty? The workings of the subliminal and subconscious mind. He knows what it takes to change someone's life. I remember the first time I interviewed him on my show, how we agreed on the same life changing principles. Thinking differently will not change your life. Saying affirmations on a daily basis, even with intense emotion, will not change your life. Now here's a guy that has made his living by helping people understand the power of thought, and he was agreeing that you're not going to radically change your life by thought alone. I loved it. Here is Eldon's story; sit back, relax and enjoy it.

ELDON TAYLOR – BELIEF SYSTEMS WIN

"Imagine that within you was a genie, a veritable creation machine capable of bringing you anything you desired-good and bad. Let's imagine that you were unaware of this genie within or had heard about it but disbelieved. Perhaps you'd tried to believe and discovered that it was bogus-the whole thing about the genie within was just so much superstitious mumbo jumbo.

We're all familiar with such phrases as "the power of the mind," "mind over matter," and "the mind-body connection." We've heard of spontaneous healing and achieving or creating the life of our dreams. Most of us have even experienced some of this, even if it appears to be in very limited ways.

Almost everyone today has at least heard of the book and movie The Secret. *They were marketed in an absolutely magnificent manner, and although they contain no real secrets, they nevertheless retold in new ways the inner mystical teachings of all ages. The Secret informed readers and viewers that one's mind was a genie of sorts, for whatever it held in sufficient detail it would attract or create, and these two words were actually interchangeable in this context.*

Maybe you watched The Oprah Winfrey Show, Larry King Live, or some other program and heard of the magnificent wealth and abundance that people had attracted using The Secret. Perhaps you grabbed a book, CD, or DVD all about the Law of Attraction and pored through it to glean the exact hows, whys, and wherefores.

Now armed with the secret knowledge and the testimony of so many, you created a vision board and printed out affirmations that you pasted everywhere so you'd constantly see them. You began visualizing all the things you wanted to attract and even started down the road of daily meditation.

You got on the Internet and looked up such terms as New Age and metaphysical. You subscribed to numerous mailing lists, tuned in to New Age Internet radio shows, and began to buy self-help books. Alas, nothing wonderful happened.

Unfortunately, that's the experience of most people who tuned in to the idea of the genie within. Some, however, found a different result. They manifested their home, a special relationship, or the like. Not many achieved this, mind you, but some. Why? The mind is that genie, and it's the doorway to the manifestation process, although its role is often misunderstood. It's an entry point, a doorway, not the manifestation tool per se. The mind provides the pictures, not the feeling. It organizes our activity to build a vision board, post the affirmations, and so forth. It invests some learned belief (expectation) in the process. Actually, the mind's highest role is inhibition.

Let me say that again: The mind's highest role is inhibition! Like it or not, we're all the product of millions of years of survival evolution. Wired in every one of us, no matter what our calling-including the most highly evolved spiritual beings now walking the earth-are primitive mechanisms that respond to primitive and sometimes rather gross stimuli. Often, stimuli that we consciously claim as reprehensible are nevertheless processed subconsciously in ways that drive us toward seeking more of the same. Those mechanisms respond to fight and flight, taboo images, socially fearful rejections, and similar stimuli in a mechanical way-thus, the term mechanism.

The human brain is a marvel of evolution, and one of its most splendid developments as far as human consciousness is concerned is the cerebral cortex. One of my early teachers, Professor Carl LaPrecht, used to say, "Whenever you find something in nature in great abundance, pay attention. It is critical to the system."

The cortex or gray matter is by far the largest part of the brain. And it's within the cortex that inhibitory power resides. The cortex is the brake. Cortical power inhibits impulses that aren't in our best interest or the result of our best intentions. The cortex shuts off the television when the content is violent, suggestive of disease and illness, or otherwise contains matter that's purely garbage. Our minds are like large trash containers: we can put anything into them. And like Dumpsters, they're difficult to clean out. Dumpsters don't tip over easily, and to clean one requires climbing inside, perhaps with a garden hose, a bucket of hot water, cleaning products, brushes, and so forth. What a tedious and nasty job.

All of us have minds, of course, and evidence suggests that when we come into the world our minds aren't blank slates, despite the tabula-rasa argument by the philosopher John Locke. No, it appears that certain predispositions and even some types of knowledge (cell memory and more) are already written in our minds when we make our first inhalation. Still, the content of our mind that's acquired following birth is the beginning of what we shall eventually hold as both our identity and our knowledge/beliefs.

You may have heard of the three components of the Law of Attraction-ask, believe, and receive. This sounds really easy until you question the degree of your belief, and that's where most people fail. I actually divide belief into three components that must be activated in the proper sequence to manifest using the inner genie. These components are:

1. The emotional input that's passionate and convinced

2. *The confidence/mental element that can simply and truly visualize something and then let it go, knowing it will happen*

3. *3. The spiritual sincerity that realizes at the deepest level of our beings that we're a gift from the Creator. Knowing that, we release our vision, for we believe this or something better, according to the highest good of all concerned.*

Anything that would distract from thinking, feeling, and knowing these three components will, in direct proportion, sabotage our efforts at manifesting our desires. Given this understanding, it becomes easier to see why some people first manifest their desires, only to lose their treasures and find themselves worse off than they were before, some fail to manifest at all, and others seem to manifest the opposite of what they're seeking. With this under your belt, you might ask, as I did: Why do most people seem handicapped by the inability to use the genie within and create the reality they deserve?

The Dumpster analogy is the first clue to answering this question. The garbage some hold in their minds would be frightening if it were visible to the public eye. As Strongheart, the German Shepherd hero of the movies, put it in his letters to Boone, "What a dreadful sight to see people's faces as incomplete as their minds." I would paraphrase: "What a horrible sight to see people's faces as grotesque as the worst in their minds."

I'd like to imagine a world full of joy, peace, balance, and harmony. That's truly difficult to do when nature seems so callous and carnivorous. As I think about this, I realize that I'm anthropomorphizing nature, so I turn my thoughts to humans, where I find such horrible acts that a lion killing a lamb is innocent in comparison.

How do we truly find peace, balance, and harmony? How do we gain spiritual sincerity and merge this with the right balance of mental and emotional stuff to manifest a world full of peace, balance, and harmony? For some, manifestation is about things such as cars, swimming pools, houses, riches, sexy this and that, and the gratification of other sensual desires. For the spiritually sincere, manifestation is first about peace, balance, and harmony and then about health and individual happiness.

These are complex issues that labels alone don't cover, so we can let the subject rest with this: each individual has a purpose for being here; and when individuals seek to manifest according to their purpose, they're enlightening themselves and the world around them.
Back to the main point: the mind is both ignition and brake. First thing in the morning, I open my eyes and begin talking to myself. My thoughts may recognize a dream or immediately turn to the new day's itinerary. The mind goes immediately to delivering the inner world of thoughts, beliefs, ambitions, goals, and so forth. That constant stream of consciousness-self-talk-informs us of our

mood, attitudes, likes, dislikes, and so much more. It's this stream of consciousness that reflects the contents of our "Dumpster."

We started this dialectic journey by imagining a genie within. I believe that this inner genie actually exists, but if you don't, that's okay. What I intend to show you is that the genie has been creating all along, even if you think that it's only some concocted get-rich scheme. In fact, the worse your life might seem, the higher the probability that the genie is working hard at fulfilling your every fear (emotion), thought (expectation), and spiritual insight ("Life sucks, and then you die"). It's in precisely this way that your hopes and ambitions are slain. Thus, your mind has been turned into the slayer.

I have taken the analogy of the genie in my own life to produce over 300 books, CDs and DVDs on the mind, success and more. And regardless of how I want to program myself mentally, if I had not risked in action steps, like investing in my ideas ... time, effort and money ... the best laid plans to create the life I desire, would lay dormant, just like the children's book character "Walter Mitty". The secret to success? Reprogram the mind, and take immediate actions in the direction of your dream."

Eldon hits it head on. Our beliefs need to be changed. Fanciful affirmations and vision boards will not do it. We are holding ourselves back. Ask for help to change. As Eldon did, take action!

Another person that exemplifies the power of changing your mind and changing your life through action, and the limitations of positive thinking, is network marketing guru Ray Higdon. I met with Ray right after the real estate bust in Florida. He had contacted me and asked if we could meet to explore what his next move might be in life. I know anyone in this situation would be anxious, especially with a family to take care of. I was excited to sit down with him and help in any possible way I could.

We met at a local restaurant for lunch, and he went on to share some of the struggles he was experiencing. I loved his honesty. I loved the fact that he was being vulnerable with me upfront and not playing games or pretending to be someone or something he wasn't. I also knew the fire in his eyes meant that he was going to be a huge success again.

RAY HIGDON – REACH OUT AND TAKE ACTION

"Although I am a successful businessperson now, positive thinking did not get me here all the way. I'll share a little bit of my story, about how I became a two time best-selling author, built a multi million dollar a year coaching and training business, and became the number one income earner in my last network marketing company. I'm going to share all that with you, but I can tell you, again, it wasn't all due to positive thinking.

I was a real estate investor in the state of Florida, from 2004 to about 2008, and did well actually. Some different partners and I moved a lot of properties. We actually owned quite a few different rental properties and things were rocking and rolling when the Florida real estate market was hot. When that market changed, I didn't know enough, I wasn't prepared, and I was over leveraged. I got my teeth kicked in. I got beat up really bad and not only did I lose multiple real estate investment properties, but I actually lost my own home to personal foreclosure. From toward the end of 2008 to all throughout 2009, I was really in a tough financial spot.

Now let me tell you what I did and then I'll share with you what I didn't do. During those times I was saying my affirmations. watching the movie The Secret, and reading different books on the law of attraction and things of that nature. I was constantly posting positive things on Facebook, even though I was in major, major trouble. You know, it's something that I look back on and it's like I was trying to kid myself to success. I was trying to ignore the pain and stay positive, but I can tell you, it just didn't work.

It was interesting when my life truly turned around. It was July 15, 2009 and a friend of mine had invited me to a home opportunity meeting, which I'll be honest, I wasn't very excited about, because I had already failed in network marketing quite a few times. When he invited me, I went there. My attitude was, "What the hell?, I got nothin' to lose." So, I went and I saw it as a vehicle. I said, "You know what? I'm not getting any younger. Life hasn't been getting any better. It's been pretty terrible the last year, and screw it. I know I'm in personal foreclosure. I know I'm dead broke, but screw it. I'm going to make a run for this!"

That is when I got into action. It is when I started doing the things that should lead to success. I started prospecting like crazy. I started reaching out to people that I knew, people that I didn't know. I started using Facebook, Linked In, YouTube, and Twitter. I started doing the activities of reaching out to individuals and that's what made a huge difference in my life. I actually went after 20 no's a day. Now, imagine this. I went a year of just writing my affirmations and hoping that things would get better, but really no action. I really wasn't taking any action. I wasn't reaching out to people. I wasn't picking up the phone. I was just visualizing in my foreclosed on house, so when I started really taking action, check out what happened.

I wanted to prospect people so I read this book called, Go for No, which I'm now friends with the authors, and they're amazing. I went for 20 no's a day. I wanted to reach out to people and get 20 people to tell me no to joining my business every single day. I did that almost every single day for six months.

Here's what happened. I created this psychological trigger that said, any time I thought about how bad life was, I had to pick up the phone, had to. I would pick up the phone and I would call somebody. I would say, "Hey, I'm running with this thing. You with me or not?" I said things like that, but I was constantly reaching out to people, taking major action. Here were the results. Within five months of that decision I was making over $10 thousand a month. Within seven months I was at $40 thousand a month. With-

in ten months I was at $50 thousand a month. That was back in mid-to-late 2010 and my income has never dipped since.

Now, not only did my wife and I become the number one income earners in that network marketing company, earning over $1 million in commissions, but we also built a coaching and training business, sort of by accident. We built this coaching and training business and we had our first million-dollar year in 2013, and we had our first million-dollar month in 2015. Then just last weekend, we had our first million-dollar event. We actually did a three-day event that generated over a million dollars in sales and I can tell you, we're so grateful to all the different mentors, trainers, and people that we've learned from. We're just so grateful for this process, but I can tell you without a shadow of a doubt that positive thinking and affirmations is not enough.

At the same time as I started reaching out to more people and taking action I started shooting videos and blogs and have now generated over 100,000 leads in the past few years and have built a major following. None of that would have happened if I didn't take massive action.

Just to bring it full circle here, I still am very positive. I still do affirmations every single day, but you have to combine action. I think that that gets lost in translation. When people see things on the law of attraction, maybe they think that they can literally sit in their apartment, or house, or whatever, and actually conjure up things to them. That's what I thought back then. I'm telling you, when you're working hard, you're on the path, and you're taking lots of action, you will get lucky. You'll have some lucky breaks, but that's what I've found. You have to be in action first. We've had a lot of lucky breaks since we got into action.

We've had people come to us, either hire us for coaching, or join our team. We've had all kinds of those examples, but none of that stuff would have happened when I was out of action. My suggestion to you is keep thinking positively. Keep writing and believing those affirmations. Keep writing down goals. I particularly like 30 day goals. What do you want to accomplish in the next 30 days and make it very reasonable, so that you can actually hit it. Keep in mind, none of that stuff is really going to change your life. It is the action that you take based on that stuff that can change your life.

I encourage you, whatever business you're in, whatever you want, there's a series of actions that goes along with that. If you want the perfect soul mate, then start becoming the person that would attract that perfect soul mate. If you want someone who's smart, motivated, and beautiful, then work on yourself. Maybe you start reading more. Maybe you start exercising more and watching your diet more. Become the type of person by action that should attract that type of person.

If you want a bigger business, what are the action steps that you need to reach that next level in your business? It is probably marketing combined with prospecting, and things of that nature. Do those things. Learn the skills that you need to learn to take your business to that next level, and you will. I'm just so grateful to be included in this book to help people to see what it really takes to create the life of your dreams."

Ray's success also has come from giving back. He loves to inspire people every day, and he does it well. Are you starting to see that your beliefs are everything? That perhaps what you want to be true and think you believe to be true, maybe isn't true at all? Getting out of denial, and looking at the truth is the most important step in the world of achieving the life that you want. His willingness to make 20 prospecting calls per day was the action step to success.

Dr. Joe Dispenza is another favorite of mine. I remember the first time I interviewed Dr. Joe on our national radio show, he was in the jungles of Mexico at a retreat. He somehow found a satellite phone so he could do the interview and not miss his obligation to be on our show. I was so impressed! He was a man of integrity. He could've easily had someone from his office email us the day before and say, "We're so sorry, Dr. Joe's in the jungles of Mexico." But instead he found a way to act and make it happen. He didn't just believe that it was a good idea to be on the show even though he was in the jungle somewhere in Mexico; he took the difficult action steps necessary to make it his reality.

I love all of Dr. Joe's books. *Breaking the Habit of Being Yourself,* is probably one of my favorites. In his books, he tells stories about people that radically changed their life through the power of thought. Now wait a second, didn't I just say that positive thinking will never change your life? And it's true. But let me finish the rest about Dr. Joe. He focuses on helping people to radically change their life through thought, and at the same time tells them if they're not going to take action steps outside of their comfort zone, nothing will probably change long-term. I remember a story in his book about a woman with a debilitating disease. She went to all the experts, got all kinds of opinions, and was in intense pain every day. She attended several of Dr. Joe's seminars, learning meditation, healing techniques, everything to do with the power of the brain, and would return back for his next seminar, sometimes with really good results and sometimes with not so good results. But here's the kicker to her story.

Even though it took over two and a half years, attending countless of Dr. Joe seminars, reading all of his books, putting into practice both mental and physical exercises to help her heal, she finally did heal. She saw a major turnaround by facing fear after fear. I'm not saying she positively thought away her fears, but rather, she walked straight into them. She did what she did not want to do. I love stories like this. Later on in the book, I will give you more tips on what it takes to radically change your life through action steps.

The subconscious mind can be an ally, or our greatest enemy. A number of years ago, I met an extremely beautiful woman who confided in me that she had struggled financially for most of her adult life. She was extremely talented in her profession, an entrepreneur who over the years had made a great amount of money but did not have one penny to show for it.

She didn't have much money to pay for a coach, but she said that she would love to pick my brain to see if I could assist her in breaking out of this rut. I told her if she was interested in achieving great change, I would help her briefly, and she could take whatever works with her into the future and hopefully apply it. Within 30 minutes of talking to her, it was easy to see what the problem was with her financial situation. It started and continued from her childhood to this very day.

She grew up in a very chaotic household filled with drama and chaos. Having never received the nurturing support needed from a mom or dad, as an only child, she was forced to battle life on her own. Her mother constantly chastised her through the school years as being stupid. She couldn't figure out math because she was dumb. She would never make much of herself or her life. These were the messages she heard throughout her childhood.

This young girl, turning into a young lady, did not get any type of nurturing support. She was not encouraged to be part of high school activities and was left to fend for herself after school hours. Within a short period of time, she was becoming very frustrated with school, and eventually she dropped out of high school. But she did have a talent. And when she found a profession to maximize her abilities and that talent, her career took off at a very young age.

She was making over $100,000 a year in her mid-20s, but every time she would talk to her mother about money, she would be chastised. "You're stupid; you haven't learned a thing from high school. You're ignorant when it comes to money; you'll always need me around. You'll never be able to handle money on your own. You're just plain stupid."

Her subconscious mind from childhood to the very day that I spoke with her was filled with all kinds of limiting thoughts, because she allowed her mother to get into her head, even as an adult. She was in what we call, an enmeshed relationship with her mother: an extreme form of codependency that she couldn't break out of. Her mother handled her banking. Even in her late 30s, her mother was still involved with everything that she did. Her mother handled her taxes, told her what to do with any little investment money she had, and continue to remind her how stupid she was in math, that she would never make anything of her own life. The best thing she could do would be to marry a rich man.

Her subconscious mind from birth to this very moment had accepted the fact that she was just dumb and unable to handle her own finances as truth, even though it wasn't factual, and it wasn't truthful. So what did she do? From her teens into her late 30s, she was a spending addict, spending thousands upon thousands of dollars every year on things that weren't needed. She didn't know she was sabotaging her own financial freedom, her own financial future. The messages in the subconscious mind, planted from birth, and reiterated throughout her adult life, were telling her that she was stupid with money. So she proved her mother to be right.

After spending time with her and giving her a game plan to break out of this terrible mental, emotional and physical relationship with her mother, the last time I saw her, it looked like she was ready to make some minimal changes in this relationship. She said she was going to find a new person to prepare her taxes. But so much more needed to be done. Her intentions were great. She had positive affirmations that she was using from one of the many books she had read, but nothing had changed. And quite frankly, ladies and gentlemen, nothing will ever change unless you take serious action. Positive thinking will not make a dent in a subconscious mindset that is filled with lack, loss, low confidence and low self-esteem. When and if she decides to do the work necessary with a professional, she can become a rock star with her money.

Maybe sometime down the road, this young woman will do some immense, intense psychological work, the kind of work we're talking about in this book, in order to break the cycle of codependent addiction with her mother and realize she's a brilliant young woman.

It saddens me to see people like that who won't or can't break out of their psychological rut. All of the workshops in the world, reading thousands of books, listening to CD's, chanting affirmations, and visualizing ourselves in powerful positions cannot hold a candle to the subconscious mind, once it's been programmed into a position of lack, insecurity, and worthlessness.

Every parent reading this book should start to evaluate the words they use when they speak to their children. I don't care how old your kids are, one month in the womb or 50 years of age. Be really careful of the words you're using. Every time we say something to a child, "You're never good at math, you're not the creative type, you've never been good at sports, you just never could grasp music, and you're not electrically inclined"… fill in the blank, we are screwing with this person's future. Wake up parents! I would love to work with this young woman's mother and get her to see the damage that she did when her daughter was young and the damage she's continuing to do to her daughter today.

In these situations, when the parent has actually come in the office and they admit, "Yes my adult daughter is stupid, my son can never manage a relationship," it usually has to do with parent envy. In this case my best guess would be a mother-daughter rivalry. It's more common than you think.

It can happen between fathers and sons. It happens between mothers and daughters. If the daughter happens to be very attractive, the mother can get jealous and try to hold her back in life. If the son is incredibly intelligent or great at making money and the father wasn't, then the father may do whatever he can to try to limit his son's growth. Don't think this is rare. It isn't. When a mother or father is jealous of their offspring, they can do some very bizarre things to try to limit their growth.

This is often called the "family cycle". It's handed down generation after generation. I wouldn't doubt that this young woman's mother was mentally, emotionally or physically abused as a child. And now she's handing it down to her daughter by emotionally abusing her. And if this young woman, that I spoke of earlier, doesn't change her ways, she'll be handing it down to her children, as well. Hence the cycle continues. This is the negative power of the subconscious mind. And it's one of the biggest reasons that once again, we want to get the message out on how to change your life now, to the masses, with this book.

Take a moment and look at the ways that you're living your life right now: your weight, your money and your relationships. If they haven't been in a good situation for a number of years, your subconscious mind has accepted truths, probably from childhood, that might not be true at all. It could come from a teacher, a neighbor, an older brother, a younger brother, an older sister, a younger sister, or an uncle, an aunt or cousins. Many have good intentions, but they planted the seed that you've allowed to blossom into a truth, that isn't true at all.

The last story I want to share about belief systems, the conscious and the subconscious mind and action steps, has to do with one of my clients, Kathy. Kathy came to me to accomplish some goals that she hadn't been able to accomplish on her own. She had been to a variety of three, four, and seven day seminars taught by some of the most incredibly successful personal growth authors in the world today. But something was missing. And she couldn't figure out what it was. She had also followed the works of many popular psychotherapists, and had worked with many counselors over the years to try to get to the bottom of why she acted the way she did in life.

Within two weeks I looked at her one day, and I said, "Kathy, I think what we're looking at is a severe addiction to codependency."

She looked at me as if I were insane. But I wasn't. In just two weeks I had found the key issue that had held her back since she was a young girl.

There are many definitions of codependency, and the one we're using here is: a desire to be liked at any cost, and approved of, and appreciated, along with a pervasive fear of being rejected, judged, and abandoned. That's the baseline that we use when we work with our clients. Kathy was struggling with all of the above. She wanted and craved affection from her core family that she never received. She was judged and ridiculed constantly by her brothers and sisters. She had stuffed so many emotions down by trying to win their approval, that she had lost sight of who she was.

Several weeks after that conversation, she committed to do the intense, written healing work. She came in totally awake and alive and on her path to healing. At the end of working together for about a year and a half, the breakthroughs were off the charts. She was standing up for herself. She was creating time for her own healing. She'd stopped putting everyone in her family first and was starting to take care of herself. The changes were amazing!

She was putting herself first, and she was seeing the benefits day after day. Her stress was minimizing. She would have times of struggle, but they would last for a day or two at the most and then she'd reclaim her power and move forward in life. I received some of the most amazing letters from Kathy, during our work together. She was acknowledging her own power. She was acknowledging all the small and big steps she was making in life. It happened because she was dedicating time, money, and effort into her own growth. Her belief systems were radically changing, but not through positive thinking weekend workshops. She was actually doing the difficult, hard work of shifting the conscious and subconscious mind. As she went along on her path, her conscious mind and subconscious mind were becoming one. It was a beautiful thing to watch.

In order to change the subconscious mind into a powerful and positive force for change, we must be willing to walk into the uncomfortable action steps for 365 days in a row. Period. Then, change can be permanent.

Use positive thinking as a springboard. Allow the cascade of positive chemicals to flood the brain by thinking positive thoughts and visualizing positive outcomes. But then you must change your beliefs. We must look at what our true beliefs are, not the ones we're telling ourselves to make ourselves feel better in the moment. To change our lives, we must do the uncomfortable work on a daily basis.

Get an accountability partner. Get a coach. Bring your conscious and subconscious minds into alignment so that you can dismantle any and all excuses, denials, justifications or rationalizations and walk the path you've always wanted to walk. Become a millionaire, sculpt the perfect body. Create deep love or save your current relationship. Deepen your path with your higher power. Release all addictions. Yes, you can do all of this, once you shatter your internal illusions and align the conscious and subconscious mind so that there's no disparity anymore. Become one, finally, become one with yourself.

Chapter Summary

Slow down for just a moment and answer the following questions so that you may get the most out of this life changing book:

1. What was covered in detail in this chapter?

....

....

....

....

2. Of the topic, or different topics covered, which point was of most interest to you and why?

....

....

....

....

3. What is one action step you can take this week, that is relevant to this topic, that will propel you to create the life you desire?

....

....

....

....

Chapter 4
The 5000 Pound Gorilla of Success
What You Need to Do If You Want Your Life to Radically Change

There's a formula for success that works 100% of the time. It's something we refer to as the "5000 pound gorilla". Imagine that a 5000 pound gorilla comes up to you and says, "I'd like that banana." You're going to hand it right over. The 5000 pound gorilla lives inside you, and if you're ready to unleash it, you can create the life you've always wanted. The 5000 pound gorilla gets exactly what it wants, 100% of the time. Are you ready to unleash that monster within? That success monster? That part of you that knows that you deserve incredible love, millions of dollars, a phenomenal body, forgiveness of people in the past who have hurt you, or anything else your little heart desires. Get ready as this gorilla is about to be released!

But remember, the gorilla needs to be fed. It didn't get to be 5000 pounds sitting inside you, because you were withholding food. It needs to be fed daily and it has a big appetite. But once we start to feed it, it's what turns the subconscious mind into our greatest ally ever. It's what takes the conscious thoughts about creating success day after day, year after year and makes them your own reality. Whatever you feed grows. Whatever you think about has the potential to grow, but what you feed, what you do helps the gorilla to grow. Feeding the gorilla is a daily action step.

This gorilla would love for you to think positively, but it isn't even necessary for you to think positively to get the life you want. Isn't that amazing? All the gorilla cares about is one thing; that you use him, that you use her, to your highest level of potential. The gorilla is daily action steps into the uncomfortable.

The gorilla challenges you to do what you don't want to do: to get up early in the morning or stay up later at night, to take courses and classes with experts that go on for more than a weekend, and actually provide support for at least an entire year. The gorilla wants you to be successful, but you must feed it. You must nurture it. You must walk into the uncomfortable daily in order to achieve the life you want. The gorilla loves this! The gorilla wants to be free, out in the world exploring, doing what it's never done before. The gorilla is our unlimited potential. So many phenomenal authors have talked about this part "inside ourselves that wants to be expressed, wants to be listened to and wants to be unleashed". Think about all of the experts and successful people I'm quoting in this book; they have all found a way to release their inner gorilla. They are doing today what they did not want to do 10, 15 or 20 years ago. Now it has just become who they are.

The secret to releasing the gorilla, is doing what you don't want to do every day until it becomes so deeply ingrained into your subconscious that it simply becomes who you are. The secret is taking action steps, into the uncomfortable, five days per week, 365 days per year.

But you're going to have to go against the grain, just like this entire book is doing by challenging mainstream philosophies. So many teachers of the law of attraction will tell you that if it doesn't feel good don't do it. Follow your feelings. Only do what you are attracted to. Only do what feels good and natural. What the hell is going on here? Can you imagine if that was truly the way to success? We would never have one public speaker in the world today! If we only did what we wanted to do, the world of public speaking would be nonexistent. I don't know any public speaker that hasn't gone through intense challenges, failures, judgment, negative reviews in magazines, on radio, and on television, emails and letters telling them they suck. And if motivational speakers only did what felt good, they never would pursue the business they are in. What if athletes only did what felt good? Or police officers? Or soldiers? Or medical professionals? Please, enough of this craziness. Do not listen to this theory any longer if you want to be successful in life.

I remember my first professional speaking engagement. My mentor at the time, the late and great Richard Gerson, had encouraged me to go back to school to get my master's degree in fitness management, sports psychology, and exercise physiology. When I graduated, he asked me what I wanted to become. I told him that I wanted to be one of the top motivational speakers in the world.

He said, "OK, get out there and speak a hundred times a year for free."

I looked at him, astonished. "For free?"

"Yes David, for free. You need to get damn good in this profession before you start charging anyone for anything."

The gorilla was awakened. The challenge was on. I was as scared as I could be, but I started accepting invitations to the Lions Club, the Rotary, Aunt Betty's social knitting group, anyone who would bring me in. I said yes, yes, yes. I was growing rapidly as a public speaker. I was understanding the power of outlines, of openings, and of closing my lectures. And then the day came when I was actually paid to present. Oh my Lord, the gorilla was on fire!

It was in Atlanta, Georgia, at a large fitness conference, and the title of my presentation was, "Men in Aerobics". This was back in the 80s, when 99% of aerobics instructors were women. A handful of guys and I lead the way to open the doors to men being involved in group exercise instruction. I'm in a suit and tie, the room is absolutely sold out, and my mentor, Richard, is sitting in the back.

Before the presentation I kept thinking about how prepared I was. The 200 free lectures had readied me for this moment. I had taken the action steps; the 5000 pound gorilla for success had done his work. And now I was ready to rock the world. An hour and a half went by like two seconds, the audience never blinked, never shifted, never moved.

At the end of my lecture there was a line a mile long. People were asking me questions, getting my autograph. I was on top of the world, and this was the life I was meant for! I touched people very deeply about the role of men breaking into a female dominated industry, and the response was phenomenal. I couldn't wait to get back to my mentor. To get patted on the back for a job well done. But life on the pathway to success is often filled with humble realities.

"So David, sit down right here," Richard started, "and let me give you a few thoughts about the presentation."

"Richard, did I do awesome? Did you see that no one moved the whole time? Did you see the line of people asking me questions afterwards? Richard, it was amazing. I think I did a phenomenal job."

Richard continued. "My son you did a great job. Yes you kept their attention. Yes the line afterwards was awesome. But let's get to the bottom line here. The first time you talk to a group, if you're any good at all, you should be able to mesmerize them. But when you get that same group of people a second time, you'd better be a great speaker. So this is what I want to share with you. You've really got a lot to learn. One hundred and twenty times in the hour and a half presentation, you said the word "umm." That must stop. Your energy was awesome, but honestly it was way over-the-top! You didn't take a breath for 90 minutes. You were showering them with facts, interesting stories, funny anecdotes … which is all awesome, but you did it at one speed. There wasn't a chance for anyone else to breathe, which is why they stayed completely still." He gave a big laugh. "You did phenomenal, but for you to become a professional and get paid good money for this, you're going to have to become much, much better."

My heart sank. The gorilla started going into hiding. I felt deflated, quite frankly. But as Richard continued to talk, I knew where he was going. If I didn't do a lot more work to become exceptional at what we call "roller coaster speaking": where you take audiences on a ride with a lot of energy, then speak very softly, then throw in a statistic, then a beautiful story, and if I didn't learn the art of public speaking and really work hard, the fantasy that I'd be a sought after, international motivational speaker—my big dream—would never come to reality. The gorilla understood that and joined me as we went back out speaking for absolutely free once again, in order to hone the skills. Three hundred and sixty-five days later, another hundred presentations under my belt, and my career was about to take off.

Now follow the story. We're talking about pure dedication; over 300 free speeches, practicing every time I spoke by writing out the entire presentation in longhand in order to look for ways that I could add stories, statistics, and that beautiful roller coaster ride that great speakers use. After two years of hard work, I was starting to travel all over the world. As a spokesperson for Reebok and AVIA Athletics, I was doing European tours. A ten city tour through England, Scotland, Germany and Spain. I spoke all over the United States of America. Reviews were coming that were even blowing my mind: "One of the top speakers of all time," "One of the top five speakers in our 15 years of conventions," "We would bring him back anytime," "Months after you came to speak to our national sales force, people are still quoting you."

From that date to today, I've probably done over 1000 presentations, but it was getting in touch with that gorilla, bouncing back from judgment after judgment in the beginning of my speaking career, and walking through the fire that led to the success that I have today. There's no bragging rights by me here; it's just pure fact. If you want to be successful, you've got to do what most other people would never do.

Remember if we only did the stuff that felt good, very few people would become the success they are today. If my mentor, Joe Cirulli, or the famous author, Dr. Joe Vitale, who were both homeless and then became multimillionaires, only did what felt good, well come on now; do you think they'd be the success they are today? If Erin Brockovich only did what she liked to do in life, do you think that she would have turned the whole legal world around through her fight to protect children and adults from corporations that are polluting our environment?

Action steps into the uncomfortable are the keys to success. Yes, I want you to think positively. We'll talk more about that later. But think about this: you could actually be a negative thinker, a skeptic even, and as long as you did action steps into the uncomfortable towards your goal five days a week, you would achieve your goals. Isn't that incredible? I know some people who always look at the glass as half empty, who do the work necessary, and create great success in life. Now I don't recommend this, but what I'm saying is that the most important key to change your body, your mind, your health, your financial situation, your love life and more is what you do five days a week. Take action steps to prove that you're serious about changing your life. And they must be in writing.

After following action steps into the uncomfortable for 365 days, whatever was uncomfortable to do in the beginning just becomes who you are. Getting up at 4 AM to go to the gym or to pray and meditate, can be an absolute bear in the beginning. But after a year of doing that, it just becomes effortless and meaningful. Your 5000 pound gorilla has just opened a doorway to incredible success. Turn around, shake his or her hand, and hand over a bunch of bananas. They deserve it.

Outside of Richard Gerson, who led the way to help me become an international professional speaker by walking into the uncomfortable, one of my other mentors, the late and also great Steve Block, the founder of a very popular fitness equipment company, SPRI Products, also influenced me greatly. He was a mentor that was on the phone with me daily, pushing me.

"David, throw a ton of spaghetti at the wall. Whatever sticks go after it. You deserve all of your financial goals, notoriety, making a difference in the lives of millions of people around the world, but you've got to keep taking risks. You've got to do things that you didn't think you would do last year. Grow—Risk—Lose—Win. But don't stop moving forward."

Steve had a huge influence on my life and my attitude, for the many years that I was a spokesperson for his product.

Joe Cirulli, who I have mentioned many times in this book, is another mentor of mine that pushed me in the most wonderful ways to become who I am today. He challenged me in the world of fitness by encouraging me to do super slow training with weight equipment. He told me that even if this training seemed weird or uncomfortable at first, that the end result would be fantastic. I didn't really believe in super slow training, where you do 20 seconds per repetition. Ten seconds out, hold, 10 seconds back in. That was totally against my "Type A" way of thinking. I really didn't think that training slowly would work for me, but Joe pushed me. That's what mentors are supposed to do. And within three months of training with him in this way, my body changed radically. I was packing on lean tissue like I never had before. To this day, I can say my body continues to be enhanced physically, on a yearly basis, because I follow his path. I did what I didn't want to do. I did the uncomfortable. I surrendered to his philosophy and the benefits paid off over and over.

Another person that has had a huge impact on my life is the New York Times best-selling author T. Harv Eker. His book, *Secrets of the Millionaire Mind*, became an overnight success, and we had to have him on the radio show right away. During the interview, Harv and I hit it off big time. On air, I asked him if he would be my coach.

He chuckled and said, "David, I don't have the time for that." I continued to push and push until he relented. "OK David, I'll give you one session on the phone, but I don't have time after that." During that session he blew my mind. He called out the go-rilla within me once again. He wanted to know how much money I've been making over the last 10 years. He asked me what my goal is. When I told him it was to double my income he said, "Why haven't you done it yet? Are you willing to do whatever it takes for as long as it takes?"

"Of course I am," I said! "Of course anyone walking this path has to want to do that."

He said. "David, that's not the truth. If you were already doing whatever it took, for as long as it took, you would have the money that you wanted. It's not true."

Oh my Gosh! Harv woke me up right then. He was right. There was something missing. "Harv, what do you think I am miss-ing?" He had to think for a second, and then laid down the line.

"David, you need to hire a business coach. It's not going to be me, but I can refer you to someone who would be perfect for you, someone who's been in the organization for a long time, the perfect match for you."

I contacted Adam Markel, the president of Peak Potentials, and he referred me on to Marleen Payne. Marleen was a perfect fit for me; we've worked together for years now and I absolutely love the direction she's taking my business. Doing the uncomfortable—paying for coaching—having someone on your side to hold you ac-countable. Someone who will force you to walk into the uncom-fortable every week, 52 weeks a year. That's what Marleen does for me, and that's what you need to do in order to create the success you want. Invest in you.

So many people say they want great money, a great body, a new relationship, or to save their current one, but they're not willing to invest in themselves. The gorilla is waiting to hear your call. It's about investing in you. It's about investing your time, money, and effort into the uncomfortable. Five days a week for 365 straight days. Do whatever it takes for as long as it takes, and you will achieve the goal that you have. I promise you. Add positive thinking just for the hell of it, just for fun, just as a way to get that rush of chemicals cascading into your brain every morning and every night. But go out there, and do the hard work. That's what all these people I'm introducing you to in this book have had to do.

Let's go right now to Joe Cirulli. I love this guy. Not only is he a multimillionaire, he has more integrity than anyone else I know. When I lived in Gainesville for a year, filming a pilot television program, Joe and I worked out every day at 2:30. And there wasn't a day that would go by, that Joe wouldn't leave our workout for 30 seconds to pick up lint that he saw down the hallway or to help someone that was on a piece of equipment. It would be a quick break from our work out, but he taught me so much by his actions. Joe is the real deal.

When it was time for me to go into recovery, Joe believed in me. He came to the plate and supported me. He wanted me to be the healthiest, most successful form of David Essel that I could be. And he proved it with both his words and his actions. I am so blessed to have someone like him in my life. Here's Joe story. From homeless to millionaire. You can do it too, if you're willing to walk into the uncomfortable every day.

JOE CIRULLI – OPTIMISM GIVES LIFE TO DREAMS

"When David asked me to write about my feelings on positive thinking and how it could be the cause of failure, I was intrigued. It didn't take long though to understand his meaning.

As I thought back on my life, I realized one of the most fortunate things that happened was finding the book The Power of Positive Thinking. From that point, I read and listened to hundreds of books on positive thinking. But as I thought even deeper, it became clear that positive thinking was more related to possibility think- ing. In other words, I could have dreams about the future that far exceeded what I had thought possible in the past. Why? Because I realized normal people accomplished great things by believing they could accomplish great things. They saw their dreams as a possibility.

Inspired at 21, I started writing out all of the things I wanted to ac- complish in my life. And, I'm not talking about the small things. You see I grew up in a middle-class family with 4 sisters, 2 broth- ers, a father employed by the military and a mom who worked as a nurse. My dreams were somewhat limited by my surroundings. That is until I started reading. It was a powerful starting point and

I started writing and putting aside my limits. The books said I just had to believe, so I did. I read my list of goals every morning and night for years. During those years I faced quite a bit of adversity. By the time I was 24 I had worked for six companies that went bankrupt, lived in my car, closed down buildings, and buildings where I worked, and got down to my last 12 cents.

This is where I separate positive thinking from optimism. Because without optimism, positive thinking remains just that, thinking. You need the action that optimism allows.

I could have given up on my dreams because of all the failure I experienced, but the truth is I never looked at it as failure--I believed everything that happened was meant to mold me into the person I wanted to become. Optimism gave me the ability to look at the events in my life differently, and believe I had control of my own destiny. Instead of seeing road blocks, I saw building blocks. Instead of having only a list of dreams, I also had a list of goals that would give those dreams life.

I knew it would take a lot of hard work and risk. I had to be willing to do what others thought was plain crazy. For example, starting a business with $1700 and hiring carpenters, electricians, plumbers, and air conditioning contractors to build it, even though I couldn't pay them right away. How did I do it? Working 18 hours a day for a year and a half, putting all of my blood, sweat, and fears into *making it happen, and putting every penny I earned to keep every-one working--and somehow I did it.*

The secret to getting on the road to success is to never look back and never believe you are entitled to anything, ever. Success is a matter of focus, determination, and a never give up attitude. Success is a course, not a destination.

There were times that made me feel sad, lonely, depressed, and the full gamut of emotions you would expect under prolonged adversity. I found that continuous forward motion kept me moving in that direction and overrode the negative emotions; my rule is to let myself feel those negative emotions for a maximum of three hours and then move on and find the solutions. I found that a period of reflective thinking followed by hard work helps me find the direction and stay with it.
Positive thinking set the course for optimism and gave me the drive to work hard and overcome obstacles. Together they built the foundation to put me on the right path to accomplish my goals and dreams and they will continue to be influential in my future."

Hard work through adversity creates momentum. Joe has made millions of dollars in an industry where people say you do it because you love it—not to make much money. Joe has become a millionaire through his three health clubs in Gainesville, Florida: the Gainesville Health & Fitness Centers.

Walk into the uncomfortable. Hold yourself accountable. Do what you don't want to do. My good friend, New York Times best-selling author, JJ Virgin, was introduced to me several years ago by another friend of mine, international filmmaker, John Biffar. JJ's best-selling book, *The Virgin Diet*, was an absolute breakthrough for millions and millions of people around the world. After meeting her, I had to have her on my show. But what happened next was one of the most shocking experiences of her life.

One of her sons, Grant, was hit head-on by a car and left to die. He was flown to Los Angeles to one of the top hospitals to be evaluated. Could they save his life? If they did, what type of life would he have? It looked like his chance for survival was very slim. I can't imagine what JJ, as his mom, was going through at that time. I can't imagine the tragedy, the sadness, the stress that she was experiencing.

While several experts said there really wasn't much hope for survival, or if he did survive, he would not return to normal, JJ believed differently. She called upon her high-ranking medical friends from around the country. She called upon as many experts as she could to get opinions. And the bottom line was this, she was going to fight for her son. No matter what it took, she was going to fight for him not just to survive but to thrive. JJ had a new focus in life, and it was helping in the resurrection of her son. But this is a much bigger ordeal than any of us could ever imagine if we haven't been in her situation before. The most important action step that she needed to take is described in the story below by JJ herself.

JJ VIRGIN - INTENTIONING

"One thing that works for me and many of my clients is intentioning. Every morning, we write our short and long-term goals. I call these "stretch goals." So, for instance, for my son Grant, who was struck by a hit-and-run driver in 2012, intentioning involves him becoming his healthiest, most vibrant self. I intentioned Grant being even better than before the accident, 110% improvement.

I did the intentioning for my son, Grant. The action step that makes intentioning uncomfortable is putting those big goals into the world and having your colleagues and friends hold you accountable. It isn't enough to simply brainstorm goals and say, "OK, I'll do them now." You have to actually put them out there and ask others to maintain your accountability. That's scary, but absolutely necessary. We then share these intentioning goals with others to gather support and stay positive, as intentions, THEY become reality.

My family is living proof intentioning works. Grant is on his way to complete recovery – actually becoming better than before – and continues to inspire others to become their best selves. Clients have shared their own intentioning stories: Reaching their goal weight, creating a successful business, that sort of thing.

Unlike simply thinking positively, intentioning involves thinking big but creating action goals and creating accountability to make those goals a reality. Get other people in your life to hold you accountable to the daily steps you need to take, regardless of the goal. That is the action step too many do not follow. "

Today Grant, JJ and her other son are doing great. If JJ hadn't reached out and asked for support, and then asked those same people to hold her accountable to make sure she did what was needed to be done to help her son survive and then thrive, she may not have followed through with all the action steps needed on an hourly basis, not just a daily basis, to make this miracle a reality. All the positive thinking in the world could not have done on its own, what JJ was able to do by following action steps into the uncomfortable. And by being held accountable by her friends to make sure they were done.

Years ago, I met New York Times best-selling author, Arielle Ford, at the Ritz Carlton in Naples, Florida. We had a really short meeting in the lobby, as I was on my way to speak at a conference and she was in Naples on business. We hit it off immediately. Arielle is an amazing woman and loves to help people understand the concept of true goal achievement. But once again, regardless of the many books that tell you that you can create success by thinking a certain way, unless it's a miracle, it's just not going to happen. Here are her thoughts on creating the life you desire.

ARIELLE FORD – SURRENDERING

"Successful manifesting requires something akin to driving with your foot on the gas and the brake at the same time. On the one hand we need to be clear about our intentions, and to feel in every cell of our body that what we have asked for IS already ours, and be willing to take action towards our goals. Simultaneously, we must stay detached from the outcome and live in a state of surrender. Now you might be thinking, "Whoa, that doesn't make sense!"

But it does. Think of it this way: When the seeds of a flower have been planted, and the first leaves begin to sprout, the gardener doesn't tug on the leaves every day to make the plant grow faster. They trust that Mother Nature knows how to grow all on her own, thank you very much.

There are many ways we approach manifesting our desire, whether it's more money, a soulmate, a new career, or the perfect little black dress. Some of us take the "if it's meant to be it will just happen" approach. Others take charge and go into "make it happen" mode. I believe that it's a combination of the two that is the winning ticket. I believe that manifesting your heart's desire has a certain amount of "meant-to-be-ness" to it... AND it requires a big dose of "make-it-happen-ness."

Practicing intention, surrender, focus, and detachment coupled with trust, belief, knowingness, and patience is the recipe for success. And I realize that this is a paradox.... How does one be both intentional and surrendered? When I am being intentional, I have a clear feeling and picture of what my desire is AND I also am detached from the outcome. I know and trust that life will continue to be great whether or not my desire is fulfilled. I surrender to divine timing and to destiny (knowing this or something better is on the way) and my happiness and well being isn't dependent on having my wishes granted.

This is a daily "conscious" practice that requires emotional maturity and awareness. It's worth the effort to master this practice as it will give you freedom to be "with what is" while manifesting your deepest desires! Those who successfully manifest have learned and surrendered to the fact that it's not our job to know where, when, or how our desire will appear. We don't have to micromanage every encounter or anticipate every detail. Our job is to simply prepare ourselves in body, mind, and soul and then relax into the knowledge that what we've asked for – wherever it may be at this moment – is on the way.

When you notice that you are in fear or doubt or disbelief that your desired outcome is on the way, allow yourself to spend three minutes or less fully feeling the worst of these negative emotions. Set a time and then dive in and exaggerate your fears and doubts.

*Make it really ugly. No positive thinking allowed! IF you do this
you will soon begin to laugh because your rational mind will kick
in reminding you that these thoughts are just not true. Then, having released the pressure of the negativity, fill yourself back up
with kind, loving affirmations that your desired outcome IS already
yours and remember to be both intentional and surrendered!"*

I love it, feeling the fears and the insecurities! No more
positive thinking covering up the reality of life! As you continue to
read this book, remember positive thinking can make life easier. It
can make life more enjoyable. I'm going to keep repeating this
concept. I love positive thinking. I just would never rely on it to
change my life. I don't want you to fall victim to that scam anymore either.

If you're not happy with your body right now, what are you
doing differently? What would you like it to turn into? Would you
like it to be a lean mean muscular machine that burns fat 24 hours
a day? Would you like to put on a bathing suit and feel proud of the
body you created? I met Tracie Cyganiak years ago when she was
a waitress at one of my favorite breakfast places, First Watch, in
Fort Myers, Florida.

Tracie had an unbelievable personality. I loved to see her
when I came in as she always made you feel like it was family
there. It became my own "Cheers bar". I ended up meeting and
knowing all of the waitresses and waiters and Shaun, the general
manager, who I still communicate with today. Tracie's story is so

inspirational, and it proves that if she can do this truly anyone with a desire to change their body can do it, too. You may not want to be a bikini competitor like Tracie, but the before and after pictures are quite stunning. How she got there is equally as stunning. Tracie has great faith, but her attitude wasn't all that powerful. Read what she had to do, the action steps into the uncomfortable, to create a stunning body that she has today, which by the way has also helped improve her marriage in ways she may never have thought possible.

TRACIE CYGANIAK – JUST DOING IT!

Before I started competing I would say I was actively working out, without putting in the work in the kitchen. I would go to the gym, sweat my butt off and eat what I thought was "healthy" during the week, and then on the weekends I would splurge. I was only doing damage to the work I was putting in at the gym. Work was stressful, I was gaining weight and did not like who I was becoming. I was in a bad state of mind and unhappy. I looked forward to the weekends to go out with friends and drink my worries away. From living this lifestyle, I also acquired health issues such as anxiety and shingles. I surrounded myself with negativity and lame excuses as to why things were the way they were.

Luckily for me I have an amazing husband who is always honest with me. After months of him pointing out to me my poor attitude, I finally came to the realization that this lifestyle was not only affecting me, but also my partner. I then made the decision to make some changes and take my fitness to the next level. I wanted to be in the best shape of my life. I knew that making positive physical changes would also impact me mentally. I also knew that I needed to set a goal to keep myself motivated, so I chose to compete in the National Physique Committee Bikini division.

Once I found my coach to help me with the competition prepara-tions, I quit all my bad habits cold turkey. It was all or nothing! I was prepping all my food for the week on Sundays, stopped drink-ing alcohol, using salt to season foods and avoided sugar. I woke up early every morning to get to the gym by 5AM. This way my work out was done and out of the way! Within the first week I dropped 7 pounds and was already noticing changes not only physically, but also mentally. I was feeling great and was a much happier person.

It was difficult to resist all the temptations of food and wanting to sleep in, but this is when self-motivation played a huge part of my success. Those cartoons that you see with the devil and angel voic-es in your head are legit, and can play a real trick on you. So if someone brought cookies to work, for example, I would ask myself, "do you want the short term satisfaction or to reach your long term goal?", or if I wanted to sleep in I would think "don't give in, you are only cheating yourself". No one else cared if I ate a cook-ie or skipped the gym, this is why it is so important to keep positive and stay determined. The most powerful relationship you will ever have is the relationship with yourself.

As I continued to make these changes, everything else in life moved right along with it. My relationship with my husband became better than ever, work was less stressful and my health issues disappeared. Most importantly, my relationship with God grew even stronger. After noticing the affect positivity had on my life, I became more appreciative of things and would pray to God everyday thanking him for the wonderful life I have. Positive thinking just has the tendency to attract positive outcomes.

Now that I have completed my second competition and shared my transformation with social media, it is unbelievable how many messages I have been receiving from people telling me how much I have inspired them. It is so great to hear that I am influencing others to make such a positive change in their lives. Like my coach once told me: "Shoot for the moon, even if you miss, you'll land among the stars."

TRACIE CYGANIAK – BEFORE & AFTER

So let's look at your life. What uncomfortable action steps do you have to take in order to radically change your life? What do you want your gorilla to attack in order to create the life you want? If you need to lose weight, what is the role of emotional eating? What do you have to remove from your house right now so the temptation doesn't exist? How often do you need to get out and exercise? Can you find a buddy to join at the gym? Can you hire a trainer, so that you have what is referred to as "skin in the game" or money on the table to prove you're serious? It's not your genetics. Trust me, it's not genetics. A University of Florida study came out years ago saying that of all the people that were obese or overweight, only about 6% had any genetic link whatsoever! So let's drop the excuses and get involved with the steps that are uncomfortable.

What about making more money? What uncomfortable steps do you need to start doing today to increase your income? Do you need to get your resume together to apply for another job, ask your current employer to come up with a plan for you to take on more responsibilities to increase your pay, or start a network marketing business? What about decreasing debt and expenses? Do you need to contact your cable company, phone, electric, water etc. and ask them to offer tips on how to lower your bills? What about the interest you pay on credit cards? Do you need to go to bat to get these interest rates reduced? What about your auto loan? What about going to your bank or credit union to see if you can get the interest rate reduced? Do you see what I'm saying?

You've got to work your butt off to create what you want. And by the way, the best formula I've ever seen for financial freedom and independence, is to get your monthly expenses to be 50% or less of your monthly income. Start working towards that today. Do the uncomfortable steps. It might mean no restaurant dinners for a year, or working longer hours, at least in the beginning. Find a way to create passive income, through stocks, mutual funds, investment houses as rentals, joining a network marketing organization. Get creative. Do the work. Release the gorilla. Become financially free.

In other words, whatever your goal is, write down the steps that you'd rather not do. The ones you know you need to do. Do them. Hire a coach, a financial advisor, a sports nutritionist, a spiritual counselor. Whatever the hell you need to do, do it today! The gorilla is waiting. And patiently I might add, but your gorilla is waiting to be released. Once you tap into that and do what you don't want to do, your life will be radically changed forever.

Speaking of money, one of my favorite financial turnaround stories has to be about my former client, Angela, from Seattle. When she contacted me, she was working a dead-end job, stressed to the max with money—not enough of it—and too many bills. When I told her that the best chance of breaking out of this would be to work with me for 90 straight days, I could hear her jaw drop over the phone. She didn't have the money. She went to her friends and family, and they all thought she was insane.

"Don't borrow money to do these types of programs," they said. "Don't put the money on a credit card, these things never work."

Somehow Angela had the strength to think outside the box. She hired me. I told her it was going to be intense work. She worked from 9 to 5 during the day, and I told her I needed her to call me at 4:30 her time every morning to talk for a few minutes, then every evening she had to commit two hours a night to networking with everyone in the world she could think of. She had to redo her resume, put it in search engines. And that 90 days from now her life would be radically changed.

Almost exactly 90 days later, after Angela unleashed the gorilla and went after all of these action steps that were uncomfortable as hell for her to do, she called me on the phone as excited as could be. I was speaking in New York City and my phone rrang. It's Angela.

"David, you're not gonna believe it! I just got a job offer at twice my income." We both laughed and I was just as happy as she was.

But it got even better. Two days later, I received another call and there was a voicemail from her that was frantic.

"David I need to talk to you right away. I think I'm in trouble, I'm really stressed out; call me as soon as you can." I could not imagine what could have happened, but when I reached her it was a blessing coming in another way.

"David I just got another offer at more than double my income, higher than the last offer that I accepted several days ago. What do I do?" Angela was going on the ride of her life. And it doesn't end there. The next day she got another call with an even higher income offer!

Do you see what happens when you unleash the gorilla, when you do what you don't want to do, when you challenge your own subconscious mind to do the steps that you didn't do before because you denied, delayed, and procrastinated for years? Invest time, money and effort into you, today!

This whole process of walking into the uncomfortable honestly began for me in 1996. I was hosting a nationally syndicated radio show for Westwood One at the time, and we had a chance to interview the founder of Transcendental Meditation, Maharishi

Mahesh Yogi. It was the 40th anniversary of Transcendental Meditation, and they decided that my radio show, "David Essel Alive: America's Positive Talk Show", was the only place that he wanted to celebrate the anniversary on a national syndicated radio show. We were honored and ecstatic!

Thinking about the interview, I can only remember his joy and his laughter. He could talk about deep esoteric things, and then giggle his way through the next question. It was amazing. I was mesmerized. But what was about to happen next would turn my life around completely.

Several weeks later I was speaking on a large stage in Orlando, Florida, at a convention. I walked off the stage only to be met by about 50 people asking questions after the presentation. But that's not the abnormal part.

At the very end was a woman waiting patiently and when I got to her she said, "David can I buy you coffee? I just flew in from Iowa; I only have about 20 minutes, and I have to fly right back." I couldn't believe what I had just heard. Someone had flown in from Iowa to interview me for 20 minutes, and then immediately fly right back out?

I said sure and on the way to get coffee I said, "But what is this? Why would you fly in from Iowa to interview me for 20 minutes? Who are you with?"

She smiled and said, "I'm with Maharishi. He loved the interview that you did with him, and he sent me here to ask you one question." We grabbed a coffee and here was the question. "David, he wants to know, and we all want to know, what you remember from the interview?"

I was shocked. I had actually spoken to my producers on the radio show about how I couldn't remember a darn thing from my interview with Maharishi. I was shocked because whenever I interviewed someone like Wayne Dyer or Suze Orman or Stephen Covey, I could always remember everything we talked about. But with this guy, blank.

When I told her I couldn't remember a thing, she just smiled and giggled. Then she said, "Oh come on, there must be one thing."

I said, "OK there is one thing. He was filled with joy. He giggled constantly."

To which she turned to me and said,"David, here's the truth. This might be hard to hear, but the reason you remember his joy is because you actually don't have very much joy in your life right now."

I was stunned. Who the hell does this women think she is? I'm David Essel. National radio show host. I live on the beach. I drive a Mercedes. I have several books out. There's no one more joyful than me, or so I thought. I knew our interview was about to end quickly.

In my defensive nature, I immediately blurted out, "But you don't even know me; how could you make that statement? I'm the most joyful person you've ever met. I'm doing my life's work."

Blah--blah—blah. I kept on defending David Essel, the boy filled with joy.

She was very kind and patient. "David, we have been sitting at Maharishi Mahesh Yogi's feet for the past 35 years, and whenever a group of us get up to leave after he's spoken, we all can only remember one thing. And that one thing is usually something that we haven't wanted to face. You will find out in the future that what I'm saying is true. Joy is lacking. I don't know how and why, but please pay attention."

With that, the interview was over. I got up and left; she went on her way. I knew she was wrong. I knew she didn't know what she was talking about. I loved my interview with Maharishi Mahesh Yogi, but I thought this part of it was ridiculous. I was about to find out something quite different.

Three weeks later, in 1996, on a Tuesday at 2:30 in the afternoon, I awakened from a cocaine and alcohol binge. I had been leaning heavily on the substances for years, even though I was helping people get sober, even though I was helping people create the life of their dreams. Then it hit me; you can't be an addict and be filled with joy. "Oh my God!" I thought, "She was right."

I started getting help right away. I went to an addiction counselor. I had this amazing spiritual awakening; the desire for cocaine was totally taken away on that afternoon, at 2:30 pm, never to return to this day. I had been blessed. But I also knew that I had been in denial. I had avoided the truth. I procrastinated on getting help. I needed help and I needed it now. As I reached out to the addiction community I was surrounded with love. It was hard. The 5000 pound gorilla within had been released. But it was only released because I was starting to do the hard work; the work I didn't want to do.

Years down the road I would walk through the same path with other personal challenges, and the solution remains the same; do what you don't want to do to create freedom and success today. I want you to remember that line. For you to create success in any area of life, you have to start doing what you would rather not do, today.

This experience totally changed my life path. From 1996 to today, in our Life Coach Certification programs, one-on-one coaching and group classes, everything is based on what we've created, called the "One Thing Theory™". We ask every person we work with to go deeper, beyond the surface mind. What are we avoiding? What do we deny? What are we delaying doing? As we help our clients go to this deep level of searching, we have set ourselves apart from other coaching programs in the world today. All coaches that graduate from our certification programs, follow the same path. They help their clients go after what the client would rather not do, so that we can release the gorilla within together, and accomplish anything and everything we want.

So, now that you've awakened the giant gorilla within, the gorilla for success, the gorilla who has been waiting for you to tap into the resources that you have deep inside your soul, we've got to use a structured, ritualized plan for 365 days to make your dream your reality.

The system that I'm teaching you throughout this book, can be used for anything; to get closer to God, save a marriage after an affair, lose 200 pounds, make $300,000 a year, find your life's calling, forgive someone who's hurt you, or stolen from you. It doesn't matter what the goal is that will set you free mentally, emotionally, physically, spiritually or financially. This program will work for everyone!

Select your one goal. What area of life needs your attention the most right now? Health? Money? Career? Relationship? Do you carry resentments that need to be released? Addictions?

Then, select the exact action steps you need to do to go into the uncomfortable on a daily basis. Put this in writing. For example, you may need to start getting up at five in the morning instead of seven, join a gym, or write letters of forgiveness to someone who's hurt you, or letters of anger to remove the poison from your own heart. Remember, we do not recommend that you actually send these letters to anyone.

When we bring these things into the written form, we are activating the subconscious mind, proving that we are serious. The more we write, the more we ingrain into the subconscious and conscious mind that now is the time to change. We are worthy of it. We're taking the time to create rituals and action steps in writing that we may not have done in the past. After you figure out the steps you need to take and put them in writing, the next thing to do is commit to a specific time of day and amount of time to spend on your goal.

So, write down Monday through Friday on a piece of paper. You can put them in columns. Every day has its own column so you know exactly what you're going to do on that day and for how long. What are the specific action steps you're going to take to increase your business, to lose weight, or to cut back on expenses? Who are you going to hire? I say this again; who are you going to hire? I know from my past experiences in life that when we make that financial commitment to hire a coach, a consultant, a meditation teacher, personal trainer, massage therapist, etc., we prove we are serious about changing our lives. You're going to have to invest not only time, not only effort, but also money to make your dreams a reality.

In our Life Coach Certification programs, we call this a specific, measurable, timeline to goals. Specific means outlining the steps you are going to take. Measurable means that you can measure if you're successful. If your action steps are not measurable, they're a waste of time. Timeline means knowing from what time to what time you're going to take those action steps. Maybe one of your action steps is to take a class that is three hours long every Monday night. Bingo! There's one of your actions steps for the week. But what about the other four days? We know for you to be successful, to turn that huge gorilla on inside, and to remove doubt, fear, and insecurity, it has to be done through physical action steps that we put in writing first. Five days a week for at least

12 months. It could happen sooner, but be prepared to commit one year for major changes to occur.

Do not trust your brain! I will say this again; do not trust your brain! Don't say, "Oh David, I don't need to put all that in writing; I know exactly what I'm going to do and I'm going to follow through." The truth is that if you knew you could trust your brain without writing down anything, without hiring anyone to help you, without being specific and measurable with a timeline, you would already have what you want in life. You would have no need for me, this book, or any of the other experts or people who share their stories of breakthrough success within the pages that you're reading right now.

Whatever you're doing has never worked at the level you want it. Surrender. Accept this as fact. We need to get serious, quit jerking ourselves around and follow a system that has worked for millions of people before you. I learned the system through my own trial and error, as well as from all these great people I am mentioning in this book, including my parents, who taught me the need to write down goals, action steps, and "pros and cons" lists. Please follow this system exactly, and remember, do it for 365 straight days in order to shatter the old limiting beliefs in the subconscious mind and bring in the new reality you so deeply desire, and most importantly, deserve.

And let me repeat this. The subconscious mind will not be easily changed. It wants comfort. It wants the known. It does not want you to change. It does not want you to hire anyone to help you. It does not want you to get up earlier. It does not want you to give up your favorite snacks at night—or alcohol—or cigarettes—or spending when there's a great sale. It wants you to keep doing what you're doing, even though it's not working for you. Do you understand that?

Write it down. Get specific. Get measurable. Create the timeline. If this seems too ritualistic, if you're a right brained person that primarily likes to be spontaneous and go with the flow, the odds of you accomplishing your goals are almost zero. If you're a heavy duty left brained person that needs charts and figures in order to go to the next level, use this book as your chart and just get the hell on with your life to accomplish what you want!

I smile as I write this, because I know we're all looking for ways out of doing what we're listing in this book. Even though by the end of this book you will read many stories of celebrities, personal growth experts, fitness experts and money experts, who use these tools to accomplish great things in their own lives. Somehow we think we can do it differently. Isn't that funny? We think that, "Yeah David, I know this worked for you, your heart doctor, Joe Cirulli, JJ Virgin, Eldon Taylor and everyone else you mentioned, but I think I can do it differently." That's the subconscious mind trying to pull you back into a world that has the illusion of safety. Wake up. I say that gently. Wake up and follow the system that actually works.

The subconscious mind will change. It will relent. It is adaptable. It is flexible. It will bend and then finally accept your new steps as its new reality. Smokers become non-smokers and never go back. People that struggle with money become financially free, never to return to their old ways. That's because the subconscious has been trained to change, through daily action steps into the uncomfortable. It's the only way that works, it's the only way that has ever worked. And now you know the truth. Positive thinking is great, but on its own it will never change your life. But this program will.

Take positive thinking and use it as a tool. Take your affirmations and visualizations and use them as a tool. But then access the greatest tool of all, the 5000 pound gorilla. Do what you would rather not do, and you will find a pathway to success that will open up faster than you could ever believe. The 5000 pound gorilla, action steps into the uncomfortable, when repeated for 365 straight days lets you become the miracle you've always wanted to be.

Chapter Summary

Slow down for just a moment and answer the following questions so that you may get the most out of this life changing book:

1. What was covered in detail in this chapter?

....
....
....
....

2. Of the topic, or different topics covered, which point was of most interest to you and why?

....
....
....
....

3. What is one action step you can take this week, that is relevant to this topic, that will propel you to create the life you desire?

....
....
....
....

Chapter 5

The Top Positive Thinkers in the World Concur: Action is the Pathway to Success

Let's revisit the purpose of this book. Over the past 30 years I've met so many people that became disillusioned with becoming successful in life: with losing weight, making more money, finding deep love, saving their relationship, or healing from a myriad of diseases. They were disillusioned, not because they couldn't accomplish their goals, but because they bought into programs that continued to tell them that they are just thinking wrong, that they're not visualizing correctly, or if they will just use this mantra, this one prayer, their whole life will radically change! But as they tried that one mantra, the one prayer, that special visualization technique that has a secret method to it, their life never changed.

I can't imagine how many millions of people around the world have given up on accomplishing their dreams: maybe to write a book, or move to the beach, or to have a child. So many millions of people have stopped going after their dreams because they bought into a program that seemed to be effortless. Which is why they were attracted to it. In this chapter I'm going to share with you more amazing interviews with some of the top positive thinkers in the world. And you'll find out they all have one thing in common: they worked their butts off.

One of the coolest athletes I ever interviewed was former All Pro NFL linebacker Keith Mitchell. Keith was an absolute joy. It was amazing to hear his voice on the radio being so calm, centered and logical, when in his career he was an absolute terror on the field as an NFL linebacker. Doing whatever it took for as long as it took to accomplish the mission at hand: to stop whoever has the ball. You can't be an All-Pro linebacker unless you have a racehorse heart, killer instinct, and the desire to be the best in the world.

In our first interview, we laughed as I asked Keith what his pregame warm-up music was, because I know all athletes listen to something to inspire them before the game. For Keith, it was the Phil Collins song, "Into the Night." He said when the drum roll began in that very intense fashion in the song, he was going into the zone, the linebacker zone. Ready to attack—attack—attack. We both laughed as I realized what an oxymoron this was that this fun and funny, centered man was recounting on our show how he used to turn himself into a linebacker terror. He was just great.

But there was a part of the story I didn't know about. Keith was actually paralyzed on the field after a hit. In front of 50,000 fans, no one moved. Keith couldn't move either. He could open his eyes, and that was about it. He could breathe, but that was all the movement he could get. He was scared. After time in the hospital, he was visited by someone who told him that the body had this amazing ability to heal if he just learned how to breathe correctly.

To a guy that had built his life around physical movement, activity, and athletic prowess, to be on your back paralyzed and told that if you just focus on your breathing, you can heal, didn't make much sense. But Keith had no option. He followed this person's advice, and over time he felt sensations coming back into his body. Could it have simply been the act of breathing? He knew he had to think positively, but he also knew that wasn't enough. He did what he did not think would work. Ladies and gentlemen, let me repeat this as a key part of our book, Keith Mitchell did what he thought would not work in order to begin the healing process of the body. What are you not doing, in your life to make the money, save the marriage, lose the weight that people have said, "you need to do"? Put yourself in Keith's situation. And then use his knowledge in your life, to do what you don't think will work. This is a huge key to success.

Keith's story got even better. Another person recommended to Keith that once he regained movement in his limbs, yoga could be the next big breakthrough for him. I can only imagine this linebacker thinking, "Wait a second, I started to do these breathing techniques which is so against my nature, and now people are telling me to do yoga? A football player doing yoga?"

Keith decided he had nothing to lose. He was combining a positive mindset, with breathing exercises, and now yoga. It was a combination of those three things that brought Keith back to life, figuratively as well as physically. Keith Mitchell had no idea that this paralysis, lying motionless on the football field, would lead him into a career as a top yoga guru in the United States of America!

His yoga expertise has been featured on ESPN; he's gone into the locker rooms of other NFL teams to discuss the positive aspect of yoga to calm the mind, increase flexibility, and decrease the chance of injury. Keith works with every day folks like you and me, as well, and his success has been off the charts. We've had Keith on the show to talk about every topic known to man, and he has been one of the most influential people in my life who is following a path that he never could have imagined existed. Keith's positive mindset, breathing techniques, and yoga exercises have led him to incredible success after a career as an NFL All Pro linebacker. Slow down; follow the path that Keith followed in your own life, as well. Do what you think will never work.

When it comes to financial success, one of the greatest stories that I've ever had on my radio show has to be that of Natalie Pace. She's the author of several New York Times bestselling books on finances and can effortlessly describe to the everyday person, the simple steps to take to get themselves on the pathway of financial freedom. I will tell you that she doesn't always go with the grain; she has her own ideas, thoughts, and mindset around money; debt, expenses, and income. It works, not just for her, but for the millions of people who buy her books and attend her seminars and retreats.

During our interviews, it's impossible to miss Natalie's high-energy and positive mindset. But I knew there was something deep within Natalie's past that she had overcome, and it had to be from more than just positive thinking. Here's her story, as a single mom struggling to make ends meet, and how she became rated as the number one stock picker in America. This woman rocks. You're going to love her attitude, and once again I'm going to tell you it's all based on action. Her success was based much more on what she did in stressful situations in her life, rather than what she thought.

NATALIE PACE – BEING PREPARED

"A lot of people ask me how I ended up as the #1 stock picker, above over 830 A-list professionals, most of whom are from Ivy-League schools with MBA's or degrees in economics. It all sounds very glamorous now. However, the lead-up to this achievement looks more like a work horse than a show horse. There is a lot more perspiration and sweat involved, than glamour.

Come to think of it, when you see a thoroughbred like American Pharaoh looking so graceful and effortless as he races to claim the Triple Crown, you are seeing just how beautiful the results of sweat equity, combined with passion, good DNA and a smart team, can be. American Pharaoh's training, diet, sleep, play, jockey, trainer and genes were all planned very carefully. It is the same with anyone who achieves anything (outside of the genes, which can be quite random in the human pool).

Heart -- passion -- plays a large role, too. As my good friend, the Johnny Lama says, "What's the difference between the gold and the silver medals? Heart." (John Scarangello is the chief inspiration/perspiration officer at Kinetic Cycling in Brentwood, Southern California.) When you hear people talk about champions, you'll often hear the words guts and heart.

My pedigree is far from polished. I'm someone who snuck in between the cracks. My degree is in English Literature. I took one math class in college – elementary statistics. I aced it and graduated summa cum laude, but no one would have thought that my degree would lead to me having a Nobel Prize winning economist and icon – Dr. Gary Becker – write the forward to my first book, enthusiastically recommending it. That sort of thing is something that you put on a vision board and dream and pray and wish for, that never comes true.

So, how did it come true for me? In fact, in truth, I didn't even have a vision board. I wasn't thinking about penning The ABCs of Money or The Gratitude Game. I was simply trading stocks on the side, trying to get ahead, as a single mom who needed solutions fast, before she lost her home. I outline that journey in depth in the first chapter of my first book, Put Your Money Where Your Heart Is. However, here is the sum total of what happened.

I needed solutions fast. It was clear that the budgeting and invest-ing solutions that were being offered weren't helping at all. In fact, if I had let the financial advisor whom my bank recommended in-vest my money, I would have lost everything, including my home. I can't even imagine how I would have picked up the pieces after that. That guy was hard-selling me to let him manage the small nest egg I had, and to throw in an additional $500/month of my salary. I would have had to stop eating to do that! I met with him in 2000 -- at the top of the markets, before the NASDAQ lost 75% of its value. He pooh-poohed all of my legitimate concerns about no earnings for five years in the Dot Coms, and was very conde-scending to me, trying to make me believe that he was the expert and that I should just trust him. Fortunately, I smelled a rat with that financial planner, even though I didn't know at the time that he was just a commission-based salesman who was trying to make his own house payment.

I made an excuse to leave, and began educating myself on invest-ing. Not by reading the Wall Street Journal and not by wishing that I were smart about money, but by reading the white papers of Dr. Gary Becker, a Nobel Prize winning economist, and asking the successful, business savvy people I knew where and how they re-searched their stocks. I didn't just follow their strategies. I devel-oped my own, folding in things that worked, making some ideas better with a few touch-ups and sidelining information that was more distracting than productive. Eventually, I began attending high profile economic conferences on a press pass, where the world's leaders and brightest minds came to discuss the world economy.

I embraced novel solutions to my money challenges, like teaming up with another single mom to cut our living, food, carpool and childcare expenses in half. That idea came from a website called CoAbode. I researched companies I thought were great and waited patiently for the price that I was willing to pay. I waited a year for those prices to occur! When they did, I put a lot of money on the line. That was August 2001, one month before 911.

You might think this story ends as a tragedy, however, I had purchased my stocks for a great price. They were great companies. Yes, the markets drug most share prices down after 911, but my companies were already very low. So, they didn't go down much further. In late December of 2001, I checked my stock prices. They had almost tripled. I sold, knowing that the recession was going to deepen in 2002. How did I know that? It wasn't intuition or prayer or positive thinking. It was from all of the economic data that I was inhaling as fast as I could.

NASDAQ went on to post 75% losses by October 2002. Since I'd had such a massive win, all my rich friends asked me to teach them what I know. They said their husbands and brokers had lost all of their money. I, fortunately, understood what they were talking about without suffering the sting of the losses. I'd said "No" to the hard-sell, but it could have been me if I hadn't been so firm and confident and headstrong. Teaching my friends to get money smart meant that I had to develop systems, which I did. I loved my work so much that I worked 12-14 hours every day for 6-7 days a week. Whenever you put in that kind of focused, passionate time improving your skill set, you're going to get good at what you do.

In 2005, I was named the #1 stock picker above 830 A-list pundits by the independent tracking organization Tips Traders. This was based upon the data. I earned that position. No amount of affirmations would have gotten me there. It was wisdom, right action and matching up something I was passionate about doing with something I was actually quite good at. I wanted very much to add a splash of green to Wall Street and to transform lives on Main Street. It is something I'm still committed to, fifteen years later!

My current track record is still in the 80% range. When I have conversations with high-ranking academicians and policymakers about my economic theories, they lean in. Their challenges prod me to improve the weaknesses and to better explain how the theories work. The true test is how well those theories and systems have worked, and continue to, in the real world, for more than 14 years now.

I still love what I do. My dreams inspire my direction, but my foot-steps take me there. Positive thinking allows you to see possible solutions for your challenges. What you think influences where you walk, but it is your footsteps, more than your thoughts, that deter-mine your destination. If you are praying that you'll reach Hawaii, but the plane you boarded is headed to Alaska, you're in for a cold awakening. People who fear bankruptcy, but try to pretend their mind is on wealth, are fooling themselves. ACTION is the biggest word in the Law of AttrACTION!

We all need help figuring things out at various points in our life. The most important decision we make in that moment is the guru we learn from. There are shamans. There are salesmen. Don't trust with blind faith. Trust results. The salesmen will rely on flattery, well-designed analogies ("You wouldn't want to operate on your-self, would you?"), subtle put-downs and even bullying. Shamans tend to be calm and supportive. They stick to facts and truth and are more than willing to show you their track record. I'm grateful to all of the gurus who supported me along the way (and continue to)."

Positive thinking is great, but as my friend Natalie proves, hard work leads to success.

When I think of one of the world's biggest positive thinkers, I smile as a name instantly pops into my head, Dr. Joe Vi-tale. Dr. Joe made his huge hit on the national scene through the in-ternational bestselling book, *The Secret*. Everyone who's ever read

The Secret, or watched the DVD, was inspired by everyone on that show, including Dr. Joe. His story was mesmerizing. I was so honored and excited to get him on our radio show; I was literally bursting at the seams waiting for the interview to begin. And he didn't let me down. He was just as effervescent and positive on the air as I could imagine. Within about 45 seconds though, I had to ask him the big question.

"Dr. Joe, I want to know, and the audience wants to know, how you made millions of dollars. Is it really possible for people to sit and visualize checks coming in the mail, or using positive affirmations as it's been told through *The Secret,* to make millions of dollars? In other words, Dr. Joe, is that the way that you made millions of dollars? Everyone wants to know. Of course you and I both know, everyone's looking for that secret to financial success."

Even though at that time I knew that the odds of someone saying that they visualized their way to millions of dollars, or positively thought their way to millions of dollars was impossible, I wanted to get it straight from the horse's mouth. Maybe Dr. Joe was different. Maybe he found a secret formula to bring money into his life. But I wanted the answer from him. I didn't want to read any more books about him being incredibly successful; I wanted to know how it happened.

And here's something interesting that I had no idea was a part of his pathway to success. Dr. Joe Vitale was homeless and had actually become a millionaire "before" he was featured in the book and the DVD, *The Secret*. He had made millions of dollars in the Internet marketing business when the Internet was just getting off the ground. Right time—right place, followed by hours upon hours, year after year of intense work. So he was already a millionaire when he was featured in this very popular book and DVD series, and once that program came out, his value as a speaker, author, and coach went through the roof!

He went on to share with me and my national audience that no, it isn't possible to visualize yourself to become a millionaire. No, it isn't possible to use positive affirmations to become a millionaire. Yes, he did use those techniques, but the real breakthrough was working his tail off doing whatever it took for as long as it took to become a massive success. Now he's gone on to become an exceptional guitarist, songwriter, and singer on top of all of his motivational programs, where he helps people break through their limited mindset and create the success they want.

Dr. Joe shared on the show, "It's going to take a hell of a lot of hard work to accomplish something really big." The bigger the reward, the greater the effort must be.

Talking about positive thinkers and people that have had a huge impact on our world, Deepak Chopra, M.D., is one of those individuals. The first time I interviewed him was in 1991 at the very beginning of my national radio career. When people think of Deepak Chopra, they don't think of someone that used to lead a high stress, Type A existence as a doctor in a major hospital in Boston. As a matter of fact, the first time I interviewed him, I had no idea that his previous life, as a medical doctor, actually forced him into the world of alternative healing. His stress levels were so incredibly high that he had to find a different way to work in this world, to make a difference, without losing himself in the process.

With that first interview, Deepak was in a hotel in Detroit Michigan, and my radio show aired from 10 PM Eastern time until 1 AM. He was scheduled to come on at midnight Eastern, so my producer called the hotel. They rang his room only to find out we had interrupted him while he was sleeping. Oh no! We had just woke him up!

My producer came on the headset and said, "So you're not gonna believe this, I just woke up your guest and I feel horrible." But then he continued, "David don't worry, he seems like a really great guy, he said to just call him back in five minutes and he'll be ready for the interview." I took a big breath. We found out later that the publicist who scheduled the show and actually gave us the number to the hotel, forgot to tell Deepak he was going to be on the air with us!

I remember one story he shared. It was about money, of all things. We talked about using a philosophical approach for people when they're struggling with money. He shared with me that the worst thing in the world you can do when you're struggling with money, is to hoard it. You must give it freely. If you don't have money to give, then you must give of your time to be of service to this world. But you've got to keep the energy flowing. When you're nervous about your financial situation; whatever you do, don't pull in, don't pull back, and don't isolate. Get out there. Get into the world. Even if you can only give a dollar at your Sunday church service, give a dollar. Or give of your time, but keep the energy flowing.

Over the years we interviewed Deepak many times on different concepts, and every time he had the greatest attitude, but did you notice something in his response? He didn't say anything about thinking abundantly, or thinking for prosperity. His answer was that if you're in financial stress, get out and serve the world, and give whatever financial resources you have, in the amount you can possibly afford. And if it makes you nervous and anxious to give that dollar every Sunday? Give it. It's all about action. By doing this, you prove to the world that you are living in financial abundance, because you're able to give it away. If it's only a quarter, give a quarter. Or if it makes you nervous to give five dollars, give five, or give ten dollars! Act—Act—Act!

Jenna Elfman came on to the A-list actor scene with her hit TV show, "Dharma and Greg". We had heard that she was a huge animal advocate, and that rings true with me. All the dogs I've had in my adult life have been rescues. Dogs that were abandoned, or abused, those were the ones I wanted. So when I heard Jenna Elfman was a huge fan of this type of work, we had to have her on my show. After the first interview, she was so gracious when I told her that I had a new book coming out, *Phoenix Soul: One Man's Search for Love and Inner Peace,* that she asked for a copy of it and then surprised all of us when we got an endorsement back in the mail of what she felt about the book. She loved it! I was ecstatic. Here was an A-list Hollywood actor who is taking time to not only read my first book, but to endorse it, as well.

It was during the second interview that we got heavily involved in talking about animal rights, and protecting stray dogs and cats. A lot of celebrities will take a platform like this and do commercials or interviews on my type of radio show, but that's about it. Jenna Elfman went much further when it came to actually protecting animals that were stray or abused. She wasn't just a mouthpiece. She didn't just think positively about helping animals, or say wonderful things on my radio show about how we need to change the way that we treat strays in our society. She went a step further. Actually she went many steps further. She told story after story of how she'd be driving down the streets of LA, see a stray dog, pick it up and put it in her car! And then bring it into her house!

It was awesome to have this top celebrity sharing how she's much more than a positive thinker; she's a positive doer. She is filled with action in this world and people like her need to be applauded. How about you? Are you starting to see all the evidence that the people who make a difference in this world, are those that take the most action in life?

Mark Victor Hansen is another one of the most positive thinkers in the world. You can see his quotes all over social media today that discuss the power of positive thinking, positive visualization, positive everything. But that's not all that Mark Victor

Hansen does, as the co-author of one of the most popular book series ever released in this world, *Chicken Soup for the Soul*.

During our first interview, Mark shared information about the power of the mind, but then he blew that out of the water with the power of positive action. He told me that he and his co-author, Jack Canfield, could have never withstood the challenges of getting their first book published by thinking alone. They went through a number of literary agents, rejection after rejection from publishers before they found a small publisher out of Florida that was willing to take the risk. Mark and Jack worked so hard, day after day, hour after hour, trying to convince people that this book would be a huge hit. They invested a huge amount of their own money and time to continue to pursue what so many people told them would be a waste of time.

As he shared on the show, publisher after publisher said, "That is the stupidest title for a book we have ever heard!"

Mark Victor Hansen and Jack Canfield are incredible examples of the power of positive action. Their thoughts may have been positive, but they went into deep action, too. They may have visualized themselves with checks flying in the mail, but what they really had to do was prove their seriousness to the universe by being willing to put it all on the line. The end result is a remarkable success story. Are you willing to put it all on the line in your life, to get exactly what you want out of this existence? We need to start thinking and acting in this direction.

The last story about positive action that I'm going to share in this chapter, is coming from a totally different angle. Another huge financial star in the media today is Suze Orman, radio host, TV host and author. When we had Suze on the show back in the early 90s as her career was just taking off, she was combining positive thinking in the world of finance at a time when not many other people were doing that.

On my radio show we always ask guests, especially the first time that we have them on, what type of challenges they had to overcome in order to create great success. And every one of them, every person you're reading about in this entire book, has gone through incredible challenges to become the success they are today. Suze Orman was no different. In the beginning of her career, just when she was starting to make money, she went away on a vacation and her office manager embezzled every penny that she had to her name. Can you imagine coming back from vacation and realizing that you have zero money in the bank?

What she had to do next is something that most of us would not consider to be an action step in the physical world, but rather an action step in the mental, emotional world. In order for Suze to be free of the anger, rage, and resentment against her former office manager, she had to find a way to forgive her. Forgiving someone for taking your entire life savings has got to be one of the most difficult things anyone could move through. But you cannot stay successful or bounce back from defeat and create a successful life, if you're holding onto resentments against someone from your past.

Maybe a lover cheated on you, or someone stole money from you, or a business partner steered you into a terrible deal, or perhaps you over invested in real estate and lost it all. We want to find someone else to blame and not take responsibility for our role in the action.

During the interview, Suze told me that it took her quite a while to totally forgive the office manager who had embezzled all of her money. But once she did, she was free. Her attitude improved, and the success that she had before came back multiplied! Here she was with her first major book contract, her first national radio show, sharing on my radio show, the action steps she took to become successful. She had to let go of the past to live in the present, so she could have an incredible future. She had to take daily action steps into forgiveness to release the anger, an anchor to her past.

The purpose of this chapter is to share with you, the type of individuals I've been working with over the past 30 years that have had a huge impact on my life. Through all of their stories, we're seeing the same common denominator: thinking positively is great, but acting positively and taking direct action steps in the area of life that you need to work on, is the key to ongoing success. Evaluate your life right now. Reread the stories from above and all the other stories in the book, and follow the path of the most successful people in life. Act positively in the direction of your dreams to create the life you want now.

Chapter Summary

Slow down for just a moment and answer the following questions so that you may get the most out of this life changing book:

1. What was covered in detail in this chapter?

....

....

....

....

2. Of the topic, or different topics covered, which point was of most interest to you and why?

....

....

....

....

3. What is one action step you can take this week, that is relevant to this topic, that will propel you to create the life you desire?

....

....

....

....

Chapter 6
Using Affirmations, Visualization and Prayer as Action Tools for Success
and A Look at the "Dark Side" of Our Lives

For millions of people that will pick up this book, this is the chapter they've been waiting for. I know deep in our hearts, we are all looking for a prayer, a visualization, or some type of affirmation that's going to radically change our lives. As you've seen through-out every person's story that is featured in this book, and believe me the stories will continue, not one person has ever mentioned that positive thinking, affirmations, visualization or prayer alone was the main tool they used to radically change their lives.

From what I've seen over the past 30 years, the combina-tion of affirmations, visualization and even prayer can account for about 20% of our success. It doesn't mean they're not important. They are extremely important. They are just not a panacea or the end all to huge accomplishments in life that many people want us to believe. Now there are miracles; someone can pray and there's an instantaneous healing of some disease. Someone else could vi-sualize themselves walking down the beach hand-in-hand with the lover of their dreams, and two hours later they meet that person! Someone else could wake up and decide to start doing affirmations and win the lottery. I am not saying that these things are not true, or not possible, but what I am saying is that every superstar I have interviewed, or every alcoholic who battled with that substance for 20, 30 or 40 years, eventually had to do the hard work of recovery. So why wait? Why put it off any longer? Why not start doing the work now, and use the powerful techniques described in detail in this chapter as an adjunct to the hard work.

I know that if you start doing affirmations every morning and every night, if you visualize yourself in the place that you want to be, and if you get into action oriented prayer, each and every one of these tools will make you feel better in the moment. They will temporarily boost your mood. They can temporarily boost your self-confidence and self-esteem. So why not use them to the maximum? Let's go. Let's use them as they are intended to be used, but let's not forget the simple fact that changing your mind will not necessarily change your life unless you do the work, the uncomfortable action steps, to make it happen.

Affirmations

Let's start with affirmations. Affirmations are statements of intention about something that we want to achieve. The first time that I interviewed Dr. Wayne Dyer, we went directly into the power of affirmations. He had used affirmations as one of his many tools to get sober, and he was sharing the power of the "I Am" meditation program with me.

The words "I Am", according to Dr. Wayne Dyer and many great spiritual teachers, are two of the most energizing and powerful words in the universe. Starting out affirmations with the words "I Am', sends out a positive vibration at the highest level possible. This helps you affirm your desire to change. And if you use emotion, deep emotion with the affirmation, you are now getting ready to radically change your life. Wayne has several CD's with affirmation programs on them that you can get anywhere these types of programs are sold. I highly recommend it. In fact, we always tell clients who are first learning affirmations to do it by following another person's voice whether it's on YouTube, a CD, or iTunes. Interviewing Wayne was always amazing; he came from the most positive perspective ever, but he also worked his tail off to achieve success. On top of your hard work, use the power of affirmations to release that cascade of chemicals into the brain, which I've referred to earlier in this book, to give yourself one more edge in accomplishing your goals.

I have used affirmations for as long as I can remember. As a matter of fact, a very interesting story came out of a series of affirmations that I used to state in the late 1980s. I had just accepted a position with the WWOR TV morning show in Secaucus, New Jersey, which was one of my greatest early professional breakthroughs. Once a week I was flown up to the studio from Florida, to be on the show talking with the host about making positive lifestyle changes. Every day I was affirming that I was a national TV host, national radio host, and creating audio cassettes that were listened to worldwide. As I went through each of these affirmations, I was filling my mind and my voice with huge emotion! I learned from various teachers in the late 70s and early 80s that it was crucial to use emotion with the affirmation, otherwise it's just like repeating a bunch of numbers. The subconscious mind doesn't pay attention to affirmations that are repeated in a monotone voice; however, we can help wake up the subconscious mind when we repeat these affirmations with emotion.

As I continued with my morning rituals of deep, emotion filled affirmations, some of the most amazing things started to happen; first the WWOR TV position. Then, from out of nowhere, I was contacted by one of the head people at Nightingale Conant motivational audio services. If you remember back then, Nightingale Conant was the brainchild of Earl Nightingale and Lloyd Conant. Over the years, this company continued to reach out to the top motivational individuals in the world, such as Deepak Chopra, Wayne Dyer, etc. and invited them to come into their Chicago studios to tape segments that were then available on audio cassettes. I knew all of this quite well because I was a monthly subscriber. I was listening to these All-Stars myself when out of the blue I got a call. That call led to a meeting. And before I knew it, I was flying to Chicago to do my very own 60 minute audio cassette with these All-Stars in the world of positive motivation. And it got even better. They teamed me up with one of my favorite authors of all time, Brian Tracy, who rose from being a broke teenager to a multimillionaire in the world of personal growth.

I couldn't believe I was standing in the studios of Nightingale Conant. It was a dream come true! All of these affirmations that I had been stating for years were starting to open doorways to massive success for my career. But let's not forget, for 10 years before that I had been traveling approximately 40 weeks a year as a motivational speaker, all over the world, sharing tips and ideas on how to break out of the mental chains in life to live the life we are destined to live. I shared tips on how to live a life of abundance, joy, and happiness. So it was all making sense. The affirmations, coupled by my willingness to be traveling 40 weeks a year, were starting to open doors that could never have been opened on their own. The same can happen to you. Let's use affirmations, statements of intention, for the weight you want to lose, the money you want to make, the relationships you want to have. Begin with the words "I Am", followed by the intention or statement that is exciting, and also realistic.

A major mistake I see a lot of people make however, is that they'll create affirmations such as, "I am a multimillionaire", when they're making $50,000 year. When we make statements that are absolutely impossible in our current state, the subconscious mind shuts down. My personal belief is that these affirmations don't even reach the subconscious mind. But if we make affirmations that are realistic and at the same time exciting, I honestly believe we can start to shift the subconscious. That's what happened with my work, in radio and TV. I was traveling, teaching the message of all possibilities and helping people remove their limitations in life. Combined with affirmations, it was absolutely working. I want the same to happen for you. Just remember, your affirmations must be backed with intense emotion seven days a week, first thing in the morning and last thing before you go to bed. Let's get into the habit of doing this together and taking action every day.

Can we combine prayers and affirmation together? One night at 2:30 in the morning, I woke up and could not breathe. I was living alone with my little Italian Greyhound rescue dog, Saint, and I started to panic. Anxiety levels were going through the roof. I had a very bad cold, and I had taken some antihistamines. I don't know what happened, but I was experiencing an extreme negative reaction. I picked up the phone to call the hospital because I knew I couldn't drive in the high anxiety state I was in, but I couldn't speak into the phone. I never thought about just dialing 911 and staying on the line; I didn't know what to do. Looking back at it now, I could have texted someone for help but I wasn't thinking that clearly. I was panicked.

I paced around my room trying to catch my breath. I could feel my skin almost go on fire as the air was barely getting into my lungs. I paced and paced and paced. I started praying, but I didn't know what to pray for. Isn't that crazy? Here I'm running out of air, you would think I would start to pray for air. I didn't know what to do. Then all of a sudden something dawned on me. I called out to my Aunt Rita, Sister Regina Loughlin, who had died just a few years before. She was an incredible role model for me, someone I loved dearly, who had been a nun from the age of 16 until 93 when she passed away.

In my mind I was calling out to Aunt Rita, to please come help me. It was an affirmation and prayer put together. But I was specific. "Aunt Rita, I need you right now." Then I remembered I had her mass card from her funeral, out in the other room. I raced out, grabbed the card and put it to my throat. I continued to pray, "Aunt Rita, I need you right now. Aunt Rita please respond." Within about five minutes my throat fully opened. For the first 20 minutes when I was in extreme anxiety, panicking to get my breath, I couldn't think of anything to do to help myself out of the situation. But then when I switched my thoughts and actually called out to my aunt, and specifically asked for her help, it was the most amazing experience to feel her love in the room. My prayer/affirmation had been answered. As I finally started to catch my breath, I could feel my mind shifting into, "I am healed. I am breathing freely with the help of Aunt Rita." All the years of doing affirmations and prayers had paid off. I was following the wisdom that had always resided within and the prayer was answered, period. What an amazing blessing!

Don Miguel Ruiz is one of my favorite authors in the world of positive thinking. His top-selling book, *The Four Agreements*, has helped millions of people take things less personally, to be impeccable with their words, and live a life filled with peace and contentment.

During one of my interviews with him on the radio, we talked about the power of affirmation and belief. I had asked him if there was any time in his life that he had faced an incredible challenge where he had turned to the power of affirmation and prayer to pull him through a difficult experience. The story I am about to share with you, straight from Don Miguel's mouth, was an absolute shock for me to hear. How he moved through this experience with such grace is a testament to him being an individual who walks his talk.

He told me that just a few years before this very interview, he was placed on a list to get a heart transplant. His biological heart was failing, and he had to get a new heart in order to have more time on this earth. As the day approached for the transplant operation, his family was extremely concerned. They were worried, but he had done so much work on himself in the world of action steps and positive affirmations, that he was totally at peace.

When I asked him how he could be at peace at a time like that, knowing that he was going to have the most important organ of his body transplanted, he laughed and said, "David, that's just who I am."

He told me that as the day for the surgery came closer, he was to repeat the same statements to his family. "There's only one of two things that can happen, I'm either going to make it and have many more years on this earth to do this work of helping people to heal, or I won't make it, and I'll be in the most amazing place ever."

His attitude was astounding. Obviously he came through the transplant with flying colors, as he is still with us here on earth, helping people today. It's an incredible story: a combination of positive thinking, positive affirmations, and years and years of work in this field that paid off in the most beautiful way.

Affirmations can help us believe in ourselves, and we must believe in ourselves if we're going to get anywhere in life. A positive attitude is crucial to have in order to accomplish great things. But, as I mentioned earlier in the book, I've met many people with not so positive attitudes that have incredible bodies, or who have made millions of dollars. They even have good friendships and relationships, but they're just not as at peace as one might expect them to be. Since positive thinking is a choice and doing affirmations is a choice, let's make good choices. Let's believe in ourselves. Let's use the tool of affirmations in order to give ourselves a leg up in a challenging world.

Visualization

The world of visualization was introduced to me when I was an athlete in high school. I would sit in the locker room, especially before basketball games, and close my eyes and see myself scoring layups, jump shots and stopping the highest scoring player on the other team defensively. I'd been introduced to the power of visualization at a very young age, and I even used it to see myself playing in the National Basketball Association. I've been a huge fan of visualization for a very long time.

One of my all-time favorite personal growth experts and authors in the world of visualization is Denis Waitley. In 1984, Denis introduced Olympic athletes to the power of visualization, seeing themselves standing with the gold medal around their necks. He truly was the first person that I had ever listened to on audio cassette, explain in great detail how we can use the power of visualization, seeing the end result of our goal, to help us achieve that very thing. So whether you want to lose weight, make money, heal yourself of a disease or create great love, you can use visualization by seeing yourself with the end result in mind.

During one of my interviews with Denis, he introduced something from the world of visualization that I had never thought about. He told me that through his work with the athletes and even our own astronauts, he started to apply the use of deep emotion while they visualized the end result. Here we go again. Visualization as an action step toward success. But it's not just sitting there and seeing yourself onstage collecting a huge bonus check from your company, you have to use emotion at the same time. I immediately started doing what Dennis instructed. Previously, in my own mind, I had watched myself walk onto a stage to give a motivational lecture. I had seen the people give me a standing ovation afterward as part of my act in visualization, but I'd never used emotion during this process!

So my work was about to change. Before getting up onstage in front of sometimes 10 people and other times thousands of people, I started seeing the end result of everyone standing up and applauding my work. I was so excited! In my mind I created this intense feeling of gratitude and excitement for the audience! This wasn't meant to be done in a cocky way, but just as a way to start to prepare my mind, body, and spirit for what I wanted to see happen in my life. The turnaround was dramatic. Instead of walking onstage nervous, I started walking onstage incredibly excited. In other words I couldn't wait to start speaking! If it was 20 minutes before the lecture, where some people get a dry mouth and they start pacing out of anxiety, I was getting a dry mouth and pacing out of excitement. "Come on let's go. Can we move that clock ahead? I want to start speaking right now!"

Denis was a huge teacher for me during our interview. And then several years later I had the shock of my life. I was invited to Salt Lake City to speak in front of a crowd of 5000 people, and it was done in a very rushed way. I didn't have a lot of time to prepare, nor did I get a chance to see all the speakers that were going to be there. On the day of the event as I walked backstage, a woman came up to me and said, "You'll be on in 15 minutes, Mr. Essel, right after Denis Waitley."

I couldn't believe it. One of my all-time heroes was on stage right now, and I was going to follow him. I thought, "Oh no, how am I going to follow Denis Waitley?" It was the only time I can ever remember that I started to doubt my abilities. I was actually getting nervous. By then, I'd been speaking for 20 years all over the world, and I never got anxious at all, until that day. But let me tell you about the coolest thing that happened next. Another woman came back to say I'd be on in five minutes, and when I asked her who was to introduce me, she said, "Oh Mr. Denis Waitley is going to introduce you. We had someone else lined up, but he would have nothing of it. He was the one that chose to introduce you. He must think the world of you, Mr. Essel."

I was shocked and instantly put at ease. If one of my heroes, Denis Waitley, was going to go out of his way to introduce me, I had nothing to worry about. As I walked onstage after his introduction, I gave him a big hug. It was one of the most beautiful experiences of my life. And by the way, yes, I used the technique that he shared with me. Backstage, I had visualized the end result of my presentation in front of 5000 people with incredible emotion. The speech went great, and I felt on top of the world for weeks afterward. These tools work. They lift the spirit. They lift the mind. These tools combined with powerful action steps will help you accomplish just about any goal you desire.

Prayer

I love Dr. Larry Dossey's book, *Prayer is Good Medicine*. We've had Dr. Dossey on the show many times, and I love using prayer as an action step, seven days a week, again with emotion. In his book, he discusses several double-blind, placebo controlled studies, where people who prayed with deep emotion for specific groups of individuals, actually helped those groups to heal more quickly than control groups that weren't prayed for. It's another powerful tool to help shift your mind and change your life.

A similarity between all the different religious leaders that I've interviewed over the years, from monks to priests to rabbis, is that they say to pray and then to let go of the end result. So use prayer as a tool, but just don't get hung up on it coming through the way you wanted it to. So we are actually praying for a specific thing to happen, but then we're letting go. We are letting go of the end result.

Another fantastic interview regarding prayer was with the Reverend Matthew Fox. Reverend Fox has written over 30 books, and I had him on the air to talk about utilizing prayer as a way to heal, and to be at peace. He told me during our interview that there was one prayer that he believes is the most powerful prayer in the universe.

"It's a simple two word prayer. Thank you."

Dr. Fox believes that if we just consistently say thank you for everything that occurs in our lives, with gratitude, even the things we deem "bad occurrences," the energy around us will begin to shift. He told me that there's a blessing in every mishap we face, and there's a blessing in everything that's going well. So why not jump ahead of the game and just say thank you constantly. For many people this is a stretch, but if we're looking for action steps into the unknown to help us radically change our lives, then as I've said throughout this book, we've got to practice that which we might not initially believe in. We cannot continue to repeat the steps that haven't worked. We must risk and reach to grow.

Pray with deep emotion. A number of years ago, I went to the only remaining monastery in the state of Florida, Saint Leo Abby, just north of Tampa. I had injured my knee and had gone in for a medical evaluation and found out that I needed surgery. The surgeon that I wanted to work with, who was an acquaintance of mine, wasn't free for a number of months. I couldn't get on his schedule. So instead of going to anyone else, I decided to wait. Because my work is involved in the world of counseling and coaching, as well as inspirational speaking, I couldn't take pain pills, because they would cloud my mind. I had to tough it out. Everything I did, hurt. Trying to sleep was impossible, and I had months of this to go through before I could get the surgery.

This was one of the reasons I went to the monastery. I needed three days away where I could submerge myself in prayer to see if any potential healing might happen. I was considering asking the 22 monks if they would pray for me, but I lost my nerve. I was afraid of rejection so I didn't say anything to anyone. I just limped around the campus with a woman I was dating at the time. I was grateful for her presence because she was helping me through some really physically challenging experiences. Just walking from where we slept into the cathedral itself was a huge challenge.

On the second day there, I decided to call out for help. I was sitting as the monks went through one of their several masses of the day, and I put both hands on my knees. I prayed with emotion.

"God, if you could even take 10% of this pain away, I would be eternally grateful."

I didn't know what else to do, so I kept both hands on my knees and I just kept praying through the 45 minute service. We walked out of the service, grabbed something to eat, and then went back to our rooms. After a little while, I asked my friend if she would walk across the street to the grotto with me, a sacred site on the monastery grounds. At the grotto, we wrote little notes to Mother Mary and Jesus, and put them into the stone wall of the grotto. Of course you know what I asked for. Some of it was healing for my knee, as well as a healing for the world in general.

The next day I repeated the same practice, both hands on my knees praying to God during the services at the cathedral. The monks had anywhere from 4 to 6 services a day, and we made every one of them.

On the last day there, I continued to pray with emotion, and as we walked to my car to drive the three hours home, I noticed I was hardly limping at all. We had to walk down several steps, and once again I felt no pain. I couldn't believe what I was feeling. I wasn't sure if I should say anything to my friend because I didn't know if it would last. The next day I woke up and at least 75% of the pain was gone. Three days later, 85% of the pain was gone! I immediately called the surgeon and canceled the surgery. That was about 10 years ago, and to this day I've never had to have surgery. The power of prayer with emotion ... and action! The action step here was driving to the monastery and painfully walking to six prayer sessions each day. Action heals.

Use these tools as a way to project yourself into the life you desire: affirmations, visualization, and prayer. Add emotion to all of them as a way to start to generate powerful energetic change. I know these things will help us, especially, when we combine them with action steps into the uncomfortable, five days a week. On top of this, find someone to hold you accountable to do the work you don't want to do. An accountability partner can be a good friend, coach, consultant, sponsor, mentor, minister, priest, or rabbi. It doesn't matter who, but get someone to hold you accountable.

The "Dark, Shadow" Side of Life

The last part of this chapter is going to be delving into the dark side of life. The side of life that we don't want to admit, that we don't want to face, or look at.

Debbie Ford was an amazing radio guest, and an incredible author, who focused a good portion of her life on helping people explore their dark side. She called it "the Shadow Effect". It's a part of ourselves that we continue to push away. The emotions that surround the shadow side would be things like shame, fear, guilt, resentment, rage and more. One of the greatest gifts that Debbie gave this world was the realization that by embracing our dark side, we are actually helping to start its release. We are owning the truth of our life. We're not covering up feelings of shame, guilt, fear, insecurity, and resentment with positive thoughts, rather we're combining the use of positive thoughts, and the reality of the fact that these emotions need to be dealt with.

We recommend that you do this work with a professional. Counselors, psychologist and therapists, life coaches, ministers and the like, are trained to provide safe passage and proper support through these processes. Healing comes not through force, but by gently facing hidden fears, wounds and insecurities.

The first time we interviewed New York Times Best Selling Author, Joan Borysenko on the show, we addressed this very topic. In Joan's work, she saw that when we submerge emotions like anger, resentment, and codependency, it can come out in diseases like migraine headaches. This was how she got into the world of personal growth. Her battle with migraines when she was doing her work to get her PhD, helped her to understand that they were created by submerged emotions. Emotions and expectations that we aren't ready to handle, or don't want to handle, become submerged. In her life submerged emotions manifested as migraines. Other people will take on addictions to food, alcohol, and nicotine as a way to not deal with their dark side.

A number of years ago, a client from Canada contacted me. She had been suffering with fibromyalgia and deep depression for over 30 years. She was on a wide variety of pain medications, antidepressants, and anti-anxiety pills. Her life had become hell. She was not functioning other than to feed and bathe herself. She couldn't hold a job. She barely got out of the house. Through the encouragement of a friend, while listening to my national radio show, she decided to take the plunge. She invested time, money and effort and flew to Florida to work with me one-on-one for an entire weekend.

After that weekend, she continued to work with me for 16 straight weeks. During this time we found that she had so many submerged emotions, especially resentment, anger, guilt, and shame surrounding her relationship with her father, who passed away a number of years ago. As we delved into each of these emotions, she started to feel more freedom every day. We combined affirmations, meditation, and amino acid supplementation for her brain. She followed our writing exercises into her long held negative emotions, seven days a week for 16 weeks. We changed her diet radically, added an exercise program, and within eight months, she was off of almost all of her medications! Within a year she was back in society. She explored her dark side, the shadow side, and the end result was extraordinary. She was alive again!

We can't hide from these emotions deep within. If you find yourself with any of these type of conditions: chronic fatigue syndrome, migraines, fibromyalgia, addictions to any substance, we want you to look deeper to see what might be causing your body to shut down. What we do not want to look at—is exactly what needs to be expressed and released. It's all about owning the dark side and expressing the shadow side, in order to release it. You can't positively think your way through life. One of the biggest mistakes we make, is that we want people to look on the bright side of life, when in actuality, their healing may require looking at the dark side of life, as well.

One of the ways that I deal with my own dark side, my shadow side, is to go headfirst into any area of my own life that I might be resisting to heal: resentment, anger, jealousy, rage, or insecurity. Even though all of our work for 30 years has been in the world of personal growth and positive action, there are many people that don't agree with me. Many people that absolutely do not like me and don't have a problem sharing that via email and text messages. So I have to deal with my own shadow side, the part of me that wants to retaliate against those who are unkind.

It is not uncommon for anyone in the public eye to have enemies that they don't even know about. People disrespect them, gossip about them, and they may not even know them at all. It's part of the process of growth as far as I'm concerned, and I know I can't shy away from the feelings within. If I do, they're simply going to grow. Whatever we try to submerge, grows. If we try to submerge our insecurities, our anger, or resentment, they're just going to take root and get bigger. Before long they will be taking over the subconscious, and we will become jaded in life, negative, and gossiping about others even though that's what we dislike most. Or, battling addictions to alcohol, food, spending, etc.

So every day, within my morning gratitude, meditation, visualization, and affirmations, I say prayers for those who do not like me. I say prayers for those who do not respect me, have hurt me, have stolen money from me in the past, or who gossip behind my back regarding the work that I'm doing in this world. I actually pray for these people every day. There are some people I know by name. Friends or professional associates may have told me that certain individuals are trying to negatively affect my career. So I'll hold that person in my mind, and I'll pray for their well-being. I'll pray for their success. I'll pray that they find joy and happiness on their path. Initially, I may feel resentment or anger, and I will write about my anger towards them. I will not run away from my true feelings.

I feel my own resentment first, then work on releasing it for my benefit. And I do what I call a "blanket prayer", where I'll pray for people that I do not even know, who are trying to take me down, minimize my gifts or sabotage my career. In this way, by feeling the feelings I have towards these people, then transmuting them into a blessing, I'm covering both sides of the fence. I may not like an individual for what they've said about me, or done to me in the past, and I won't shy away from those feelings, but at the same time I need to rise above them and pray for their success in this world. I feel my own resentment towards these individuals, and then I end my morning session with prayers for them. This practice has served me well over the years.

Friends and family members are often times amazed when they bring up the name of someone who's hurt me in the past or maybe even in the present and I just smile about it. They say to me, "How come you're not angry that this person said this again?" To which I'll say, "That's the power of having a ritual on a daily basis, not monthly, but a daily basis to deal with our dark side. The side that we'd rather not look at. I'm more interested in my own emotional freedom, and slowly releasing resentments and anger, then I am about being right." This type of attitude and daily exercise, can help all of us in life. Consider trying it today.

Never give up. Never lose hope. Never lose faith. Reach out and ask people for help. That is one of the most proactive, positive moves that you could ever do. I can tell you right now, and I know you understand this by reading this book, that I have had a number of people as mentors, teachers, and coaches. These people have helped pull me out of some of the most amazingly deep, narrow, dark places in my own life: addiction, bankruptcy, and divorce. Just like you, I faced that darkness. Deep clinical depression, suicidal thoughts, all of these I own today and speak about without shame or guilt. They're just part of David Essel. Let's do the work to become free. Then, a positive attitude combined with doing the work you would rather avoid, can set you free. It's time to rock!

Chapter Summary

Slow down for just a moment and answer the following questions so that you may get the most out of this life changing book:

1. What was covered in detail in this chapter?

....

....

....

....

2. Of the topic, or different topics covered, which point was of most interest to you and why?

....

....

....

....

3. What is one action step you can take this week, that is relevant to this topic, that will propel you to create the life you desire?

....

....

....

....

Chapter 7

Beyond Positive Thinking to Positive Living:

You Just Might See Yourself Somewhere in this Chapter

This chapter is all about people that went from positive thinking to positive living, by leading a life of positive action. And you just might find yourself in one of the stories. The examples that I'm about to share are from several of my clients, who I've seen blossom into limitless, positive human beings. As you have already guessed, they did it by making a decision to do what they would rather not do. They did this on a daily basis by taking uncomfortable action steps that would lead them to a radically different, powerful, and positive life change. Challenging daily tasks, that were at one time difficult for them to complete, simply became an effortless part of their daily life. They went from periodic positive thinkers, to positive doers. They all went way beyond the realm of positive thinking to positive living. You can do the same.

Lynn is one of many individuals we worked with over the years that had spent huge amounts of money on addiction recovery and the best treatment centers. She never found the sobriety that she so desperately wanted. In her case, after spending $200,000 on her recovery, she had just about given up. She went to her final treatment center, into the detox unit, and came out a number of days later unsure if she was going to be able to pull this off—to let go of alcohol and prescription drugs. She had been relying on them for over 20 years, and even though she was fresh out of a treatment facility, she had no confidence that she could do it this time or that this time would be any different than the past.

A friend of hers recommended my work. She had worked with me on her own recovery and knew that Lynn could benefit greatly. Why? Because we do it differently. I know everyone says that, but here are Lynn's words about the power of our holistic addiction recovery program.

"After spending over $200,000 on treatment centers for my addictions, the results were never long-lasting. Finally, I found complete recovery through David's holistic addiction recovery program. David reaches into the areas of emotional and physical recovery, including brain chemistry, which no one else does. My whole family is indebted to his work."

With Lynn, we started off with the emotional work. Everyone says they do this, but not everyone does. The core of her addiction and the core of all addictions, is codependency in one form or another. As we examined her past, we saw an extreme codependent nature, the willingness and desire to put everyone else's needs first, which is so common in the world of addiction. Lynn's addictions were to alcohol and drugs. People with untreated codependency can resort to sex, emotional spending, food, or nicotine as a way to feel better in the moment, as a way to cover up their feelings of lack, their feelings of worthlessness—it's all the same thing.

It's unfortunate that too many treatment programs do not utilize brain chemistry supplements in order to help the brain begin to regain normal functionality.. And very few that I've ever spoken to, utilize the intense work that we do in the world of codependency. Lynn has told me over the past year and a half that we have worked together, that understanding her addiction to codependency was something no one else had ever approached her with.

I am so proud of her, for the intense work she's done with our program. She's never backed away from one exercise I've asked her to do, one book I recommended that she read, or one supplement that I recommended she use. She has been 100% in the game from the beginning, and her recovery is a great example of her work. Positive attitude? Heck yes! Positive work ethic? That's what sets her apart, and it's the reason she's clean, sober and happy today.

Another great example of the power of positive action in recovery, comes from another former client, Jim. Jim was a thirty-year functioning alcoholic; meaning that he held a job and never missed work, while drinking to excess. He relied on alcohol every day to get him through his existence. As a waiter, he was serving alcohol all evening long, and at the end of the evening, it was very common for the wait staff to get together and have a few drinks before they went home. But that was never enough for him. Upon arriving home, he would crack open another bottle of vodka and drink until the early morning hours.

Some people ask, "Is that really functioning?" The definition we use for functioning, is someone who's able to work, pay mortgage payments, car payments, and are responsible enough to meet their basic survival and physical needs in life. It's been eight years now, and Jim is still working in the same environment and still sober. The reason for his success? Just like Lynn, Jim surrendered 100% to our program. Whatever exercises we gave him to do, both within our program as well as attending outside meetings for his recovery, he did with 100% effort. He followed the exact program we created for him individually, knowing his needs and wants, and he is a success today and an incredible role model for others. He had to do what he would rather not have done in the beginning, but then that just became a part of his daily life.

Several of our clients that I'll talk about in this chapter, were going after success in multiple areas of their lives. April is one of those people. She came to me to become a Certified Master Life Coach, excited about the opportunity to help people change their lives. A former teacher and stay at home mom, April was determined to do something new with her life and make a big difference in this world. After graduating from the course, she became filled with doubt. I would get calls every few months from her.

"David, I just don't see enough clients coming in. The people I'm working with are doing great, but I don't see the flow I need."

I would reassure April. "It takes time to build your own business; you're an entrepreneur now. Three to five years is normal; keep moving forward. I'm here for you when you need me."

The following year, I would hear from April from time to time, sometimes with great stories of success, other times with doubt. But as another year or two went by, I heard from her less and less. She was becoming a rock star! When her first book was published, I was more excited than anything. Then she decided to create the "Happy Mom's Conference," where she brought in experts from around the USA to help moms live a more successful life. April was taking off in her career in the most magical ways imaginable. Then came her second book.

Today, she is a business coach for women who have their own businesses and want to go to the next level. And along the way, through the work we did in the life coach certification, she's actually enhanced her marriage. April and her husband now have a relationship far greater then it was the very first time I met her a number of years ago. And how are the two related? When you take care of yourself and follow your own dreams, you start to see your partner in a different light. At first it can be threatening to any relationship or marriage. But over time, if you're doing the deep emotional work that April did on herself, you start to create changes in the way you look at your partner. It's been beautiful to watch her blossom in not only her career, but her marriage.

Years ago, Marilyn contacted me after struggling with weight for most of her life. In over 30 years she had gained in excess of 120 pounds and had taken all of the available courses to help her lose weight. She joined all the weight-loss groups, the clubs, the organizations. But nothing worked. A friend of hers was listening to my national radio show, heard me talk about our weight-loss programs and asked Marilyn to contact me.

After working with her for about eight weeks, I laid it on the line. "Marilyn, if you're willing to do everything I ask of you, you will be successful in losing the 120 pounds. But there can't be excuses. When the winter hits in the Northeast, I'm still going to ask you to get outside and do your exercises. I'm still going to ask you to move away from your comfort foods to the clean diet that we are working on right now. Marilyn, if you want that, you can have it, but you have to stop making excuses."

She knew by now, not to take these comments personally as I was simply being honest with her. Her great reward, losing the 120 pounds that she had carried for over 30 years, could only come off if she surrendered to this program. And she did. Twelve months later to the day, she had lost 120 pounds! Her attitude was off the charts. Her action steps, doing what she did not want to do with her diet and exercise program, lead to a positive mindset and positive life change.

Let me repeat that. So many people think that you have to have a positive mindset first in order to create positive action steps. But we know that's not true. If you do the positive steps in your life today that you need to do, in this case regarding diet and exercise, and you start to see the results you've always wanted, the natural inclination of the brain is to start to feel better about yourself! When you have an increase in self-esteem and self-confidence through weight loss, you automatically start to think more positively. Marilyn is a great example of this. Through the harsh winters of New England, she never missed a day of outdoor exercising. No matter how many parties she went to, where all they had were comfort foods, Marilyn got used to bringing her own food to the party. Twelve months and 120 pounds later, Marilyn was a totally different person.

Thanks to the invention of programs like Skype, our coaching business has exploded around the world over the last 15 years. Marianne, from Australia, contacted me originally because of frustration with men.

"David, there just are no good men left in Australia, or New Zealand, or anywhere around my geographical area."

I've heard this millions of times. I've worked with women who live in Manhattan who say there's no available men in New York City. I shake my head and know that there's a deeper reason for this lack of availability then the actual lack of men who would be interested in a relationship. As Marianne and I worked together more, we started to find the core of the issue. When she was a really young girl, she was sexually molested by her father. Comments were made, which made her uncomfortable as she blossomed into a young woman. A touch here or touch there that felt inappropriate, resided in her subconscious, and unbeknownst to her, led to a distrust in men. And for a very good reason.

Many times, when at the subconscious level we do not trust men, we may be attracted to men that are not trustworthy. Why? It's our "comfort zone". It's what we know. Remember that "comfort zones" are not always healthy; they are simply what we know the most about.

As our work continued to become more and more intense, she started to see the reality. All the men that she chose to date were emotionally unavailable, and this was due to the fact that she grew up in a home where her father was emotionally unavailable. He was an abuser. That was her role model growing up. We had her begin by writing weekly letters to her father, which she never gave to him, to release the anger and rage inside. She was amazed at the emotion that was lurking deep within. At first she felt guilty and even ashamed that she was writing such anger riddled letters to her own father. But once she became comfortable with it, she was ready to move on. Then came letters of forgiveness: forgiveness to herself for not dealing with this before she had reached the age of 50, and letters of forgiveness to her father, for whatever drove him to say the inappropriate things he said, and to touch her in ways that were totally disrespectful. She was healing and healing fast.

After committing over 10 weeks to this intense work via Skype, she was feeling the desire to go out into the world of dating once again. I had shared with her that she'll know if the healing has actually taken place, if she leaves unhealthy relationships early. Isn't that an oxymoron? In other words, when we're healed from past hurts that hold us back emotionally, in regard to relationships, one of the ways we know we're healed is that we are able to sense men or women who are emotionally unavailable, or physically unavailable, and we leave the relationships without having to go any further. She had become an expert at what we term, "machete dating." Machete dating is when we know for sure that someone is not a match for us, and instead of being needy or lonely and hanging onto someone who isn't good or healthy for us, we cut the ties quickly. As she let go of all these emotionally and physically unavailable men before she became attached, her confidence started to soar. Her self-esteem was at an all-time high. And she was ready for the love of her life.

Every once in a while, we will have an intense spiritual experience in a session with a client. One of the most profound ones happened around the year 2000, when a brand-new client named Ardith, came walking into the room. I say prayers and intentions before every session, asking to be guided to ask the right questions, and to give the right assignments, so my clients can heal as quickly as they are supposed to. Ardith came in and was filled with pain. She lost her best friend, her mother, and she didn't know what direction to take in her life. Should she stay in the town she's living in? It was filled with boring people. There didn't seem to be very many people she could connect with. She was torn, experiencing the pain of loss, and questioning her future.

As I sat there feeling the energy of her pain, I sent out a quick prayer. Within seconds the most amazing thing happened. Ardith was expressing her pain and confusion and suddenly all around her, lightning bolts were filling the room! It was the most profound energetic experience I have ever had in my life. Over the years I've had many clients comment to me, or write to me, that the aura or energy field around me and behind me, expanded as the session went on. In other words, it's not uncommon for clients to report that they see light behind me in the office while we're doing our work. But this is one of the few times that I saw this happening behind the client. It wasn't very long before these lightning bolts of energy were filling the whole room. In that moment, I saw the most amazing explosion around my client, and this big smile of relief came across her face. It was a beautiful revelation for her to express all the pain that she had been carrying, both about the loss of her mother and about the confusion of her life purpose, in a non-judgmental environment.

Within just a few weeks she was a totally different person. There was no more talk about leaving her city. She was becoming more content. Then she reached out to a local church and started to do volunteer work. This turned into a full-time position, organizing a series of lectures with ministers from around the world whom she invited to come and speak to her congregation. What a beautiful transformation that quite honestly happened in a one hour session. I will never forget that day or how wonderful a friend this person has become to me.

Another client that has seen immense growth in a variety of areas of her life is Patti. Patti came to me after years of struggling with alcohol, and after 12 months of being in our holistic addiction recovery program she was on her way to total healing. It was so amazing to see the shifting of her energy, the beauty that came out around her face, when she was free of a substance she relied on for years. Her relationship also improved dramatically!

Many positive things happened quickly in her life, and she decided to contact me again. This time it was about financial freedom. She was an emotional spender, buying gifts for people that kept her in financial handcuffs. She would also go to the grocery store two, three or four times a week to pick up one item, only to walk out with $40 or $50 worth of products. When you add up these daily expenses over the course of 30 days or 12 months, you can easily see that regardless of how much money you make, you could find yourself in a financial bind. So Patti and her partner took my financial freedom course, and within three weeks she was at her bank, negotiating her car lease. Then, we put her on a budget for groceries. Next I had her go into her financial planner's office to redirect her investment funds.

At first Patti was nervous and resistant, but she did the work anyway. Read this again. At first she was nervous—even insecure to talk to anyone regarding money—but she did the work anyway. Her reward for walking into the uncomfortable was instantaneous. In a quick visit to the bank, she was able to redirect her car loan and save over $100 a month. Within a short time, she was saving $300 to $400 a month on groceries. A little while later, Patti was being asked by her girlfriends to help guide them into financial freedom. I love to see these type of turnarounds. But the only way Patti became sober, was to do everything we asked her to do without question. We know our program works, and she followed it step-by-step. Then she became financially free by following the sometimes uncomfortable steps that we give our clients through that program. Amazing. Rewarding. And of course you can imagine, along the way her attitude improved, as well.

Over the past five years, the number of men that are coming into our program for help in their relationships has increased dramatically. There are more and more men who are starting to look in the mirror and see that they are bringing a lot of negative traits from one relationship into another. This is decreasing their chances of finding long term, stable love. John was one of those people. In his marriage he cheated and lied, and then he was put "on the cross" by his former wife. Regardless of how many times he apologized, it was never enough. Because of this experience, he became filled with shame and guilt. When you marry low self-esteem with shame and guilt, you're asking for a myriad of challenges in any future relationship, which is what John found.

He began by forgiving his former wife, then former girlfriends, and then the biggest trial of all for John was to forgive himself for the ways he had mistreated people, especially the women in his life. He had lied to some of them, cheated on others. At first it seemed impossible to forgive himself for all of those actions.

I remember one day when he asked me, "David, aren't I supposed to feel guilty and ashamed for what I've done in the past for the rest of my life"?

It's a great question. And the answer is hell no! Once we come to the realization that we've hurt others, we need to apologize for our wrongs. This can be done in letters that are never given to those we've hurt. That's a decision that we make with each client. And the next move is to forgive ourselves. We can remove all shame, guilt and remorse when we truly forgive ourselves—when we own the errors of our past. John is now on his way to being ready for an incredible, deep, loving relationship. He's done the work. I love to see his progress. He's become more confident, calm and compassionate. And he's done it by doing the work for over six straight months in a row: every week, answering every question in writing; doing the research necessary, to see why he did what he did in the past; and turning it around.

After being married for 20 years, Betty and Daniel ran into a problem they never expected to experience in life. Daniel had strayed. He had an affair. And Betty had no idea what to do about it. Her friends and family advised her to divorce him immediately, but she came into the office unsure that this was the correct path to take. After working with her for about a month, one day she made a declaration that she asked to keep confidential, since she knew I was working with her husband, as well.

"David, I'm going to fight like hell for this marriage. I know everyone thinks I'm crazy, but I'm making this commitment today, I am not letting him go. I know we can turn this around."

I was so excited to see the expression on her face, through her tears, saying she wanted to fight for her marriage. The next day her husband Daniel came in for his session. They barely spoke during the first four to six months that I worked with them individually. Daniel was not sure he wanted to return to the marriage. He also wasn't sure if he wanted to stay in a relationship with the woman he was having an affair with. But something magical happened the day after Betty made the decision to fight for the marriage.

Daniel looked at me and said, "David, I know all the written exercises you're giving me are to help me get off the fence. To make a decision. But for months now I haven't come close to making that decision. Something weird happened last night in my sleep, and I woke up today saying that I've got to fight for my marriage. I don't know where it's coming from; will you help me figure out a path in order to win my wife back?"

It was so incredible to see that somehow energetically, these two people had separately made a decision to fight for their marriage. But I want to tell you, it wasn't easy. I worked with them for over a year until they were able to release the past and look towards the future. It was 10 years ago that I worked with them on this very problem, and I still hear from them periodically. When they do contact me, it's always about something ecstatic.

"David our marriage is stronger than ever. It's been 10 years since we worked with you; we're not sure what process you used, but it worked. We are more in love now that we've ever been in our entire life together."

The work that I do with couples, which involves an affair, is usually done separately. I don't really believe in couples counseling and I haven't since 1996 when we created our own methodology for counseling and coaching. Our system works. This is only one of many examples of couples we've helped recover from affairs. It's up to the couple to do all the work we give them, in order to recover their love.

The final story for this chapter has to do with one incredible woman named Rita. I've worked with Rita for several years now, on many different areas of her life. But the last two years have been the most magical. After not working together for about two years, she came back wanting to grow her business. Most people would comment about her industry this way. "You do it because you love it, but you don't make a lot of money." Rita was tired of that. By working together for 12 straight months, we created a game plan, a business plan that flourished in ways that neither of us would ever have guessed. She branched into a unique, specific area in the world of fitness, to create a name for herself. This has paid her back in the most beautiful ways financially and enhanced her purpose in life. But it didn't stop there.

After getting her business up and running at an exceptional level, we started to work on her relationships. Codependency was a main theme here, too. Staying with people that weren't on the same level was a common thread. Wanting to help people, seeing the good in them and saving them, is a trademark of many people that struggle with codependency.

Dating people "for their potential" is a pitfall of the codependent lover. Rita and I spent a good portion of another year working on this area of her life. I could see her progressing quickly. I'm sure it didn't seem very fast to her, but when you have a client holding onto traits like codependency for 20, 30 or 40 years, and you see them starting to change in a period of six or eight months, that's fast!

It wasn't long before she met a truly incredible guy. After spending a little bit of time with him she came to one of my seminars on love and relationships, and the most beautiful thing happened next. Within 48 hours she was engaged. Was it the seminar? Heck no. But it was just one of the many action steps that she took, proving to herself and the world that she was ready for deep love. Her partner sensed it, picked up on it, and asked her to be with him for life. It was a beautiful story in her business life, and now in her personal life, too.

So what do all of the successful people have in common? They all invested time, effort and money into themselves. And for some of them, this was the first time they ever put such a commitment into their own personal growth, business growth, and happiness. They all did the homework weekly. They stayed positive every day even through doubt, using the tools we give our clients so they thrive, not just survive.

Through weekly accountability and encouragement from myself, we've been able to help thousands of people, just like the ones mentioned above, to create the life of their dreams. Accountability is the key. Encouragement runs second. At some point they all decided to fully surrender to the program.

They had to make a commitment to do what they did not want to do in order to see success. And 100% of the time when they followed this method, they were successful.

You are no different than anyone in this book. You can shatter your own limited reality and create the life you desire. What you want is possible. But, it will take a lot more than thinking positively. Positive thinking is wonderful, but positive action leads to the results you desire.

How are all of these former clients so incredibly successful? The answer is simple—they were all willing to do whatever it took for as long as it took—and you have the same capability! Every coaching or counseling program is unique. Why? Because they are dependent upon the person you are working with, and every coach or counselor has a unique set of skills that makes them successful in their desire to help others in life.

Our program is exceptionally unique because of two distinct reasons:

1. Since 1990, we have offered a 100% money-back guarantee on every program we have created.

2. We create a totally different plan or program for each person, regardless of what goal they might have. Because each person is different, there's no cookie-cutter work here, our system releases the deep internal blocks so that you can be successful, without our help later on in life. And that's crucial. The coaching program should free the individual and teach them such powerful tools so that they don't need a coach, counselor, or program anymore.

Let's take a closer look at number one, and yes it's one of our company's most powerful action steps that has helped us grow annually for over 25 years. In 1990, we started offering every client a 100% money-back guarantee. If you do all the work that we set up for you, and you do not feel you got your money's worth, or that you didn't see some type of incredible life change, we will give your money back. No questions asked. Ever. Since 1990, there has never been one individual, who has completed the program that asked for their money back. Not even one. No one has ever come back to us after working together for eight weeks, 12 weeks, a year, or longer and said, "David, this was a lot of fun but it didn't work for me." Every person sees massive change and massive success, when they're willing to do the work. This is a track record were incredibly proud of—and it will continue until we leave this planet.

We also have a 100% success rate. Who else can say that? A 100% success rate with our clients. And it's for the same reason, every person that comes into our program who does the work will be successful. And many times they're going to be more successful than they ever imagined possible. It is not uncommon for someone to come to us to become financially free, and then decide to stay a little longer to get sober, and then stick around to find the love of their lives! Some will decide to forgive someone who hurt them 20 years ago or to find a deep meaningful spiritual path or to open up a new business. In other words, many clients are so excited when they see the initial success in just one area of their lives, they keep coming back for more. This is so rewarding to me and to our staff, to see these individuals at the end of 12 or 16 months, radically changing every area of their existence. It's also the reason that I will never retire. I will do this work until they lower me into the ground—I won't even stop there!

Now let's explore, a little more deeply, the second point that makes our program so unique. The plan that we set up, is to help people remove the internal block that keeps them stuck, on the fence, and frustrated in life. And every person is different. If we work with two different people on weight loss, the odds are they will be doing fairly different programs in order to become success-ful. And why is that? It's because of the subconscious mind, the in-ternal beliefs that lead them to begin working with us in the first place. It's very rare for us to work with individuals, and to see two people with the same issue that have identical subconscious blocks or the same limiting belief system. There is no cookie-cutter approach to our program, and there really shouldn't be with anyone's program. The more unique we make it for you, the quicker you will find success in life.

Within our programs, we help people find out what their true beliefs are, not just what they want them to be. And this is crucial! Your true beliefs are actually reflected back to you in your own life. Let me repeat this crucial lesson about belief systems. Look at the last 10 years. If you say to yourself that you're living a life of abundance and prosperity, and you are financially worthy of making $100,000 per year, all you have to do is look at the last 10 years of your life to see if those beliefs are accurate or not.

If you say your belief is that you're ready for deep love, and you've done the work over the last 10 years to remove the blocks, the insecurities, or whatever might be holding you back, yet all you have seen is chaos and drama in love, then the belief that you were hoping was true, that you're ready for deep love, probably isn't true or you would be experiencing deeper and deeper relationships along the way.

For each individual, we create specific written, physical and emotional assignments to find the blocks and remove them once and for all. We will help you answer questions like the following: What is your resistance to change? What subconscious beliefs are holding you back? Could it be that you do not feel worthy of success in this area of life? Is there a fear of success? A fear of failure? A fear of being judged? Regardless of how you dress or present yourself in public, is there a lingering insecurity that's holding you back? Could it be shame, guilt, grief, resentment or rage?

Sitting and asking yourself these questions is a very difficult thing to do. Being honest with yourself in answering these questions is even more difficult to do. That is why you need an outside system—an unbiased system—one which we have created —that helps you get to the core of every individual block and remove it for good.

We find one huge weak link and heal it, remove it, and replace it with action steps so that you can become unlimited. Our 100% money-back guarantee proves that we know what we are doing. This system has worked for a very long time.

The end result is that we help you align the conscious and subconscious mind so that what you desire, which is within the conscious mind, is firmly planted within the subconscious mind, so that you can create the life that you want in your own physical world.

If your conscious and subconscious mind are not fully aligned, you will dance back-and-forth in life. You might see great amounts of change in your income for a year, or two years, and then it goes sliding back down to the bottom for the next year or two.

You could see the weight come off, and then back on, the familiar yo-yo weight loss, weight gain scenario that tells me the conscious and subconscious mind are nowhere near fully aligned.

But when you're able to marry the conscious and subconscious minds together, and have your conscious thoughts become deeply implanted into the subconscious mind, you're able to rock this world! Then it becomes effortless to get up at 4 AM to do what needs to be done or to look your partner in the eyes and say, "I'm sorry, I won't do that again." And you actually never do it again. Interesting thought isn't it?

When the conscious and subconscious mind are aligned, we're filled with integrity. We walk the talk. We do what we say we're going to do. We would never promise anyone in this world something that we wouldn't follow through with, unless an emergency got in our way. And here's the kicker. We would never promise ourselves that we're going to do something positive in our life, and then not follow through. When our conscious and subconscious minds are aligned, and we say we're going to start a meditation program, quit smoking, quit drinking, start exercising, or drop emotional spending, we then find a program to follow and do what we told ourselves we were going to do. No more New Year's Eve resolutions that continue to be repeated 10 years in a row. That's the past. The new present—with conscious and subconscious minds in alignment—means we simply do what we say we're going to do. It's an exciting way to live. You can sleep at night. Your self-esteem, self-love, self-confidence, and your ability to go after what you want in life, become totally aligned.

If there's anything I want you to remember, it's that taking the action steps and investing time, money, and effort into yourself

—whatever your goal might be—is the key to living a life on purpose. Once you do this, your attitude instantaneously changes. If
you are a strong positive thinker today, add action steps in order to
bring your life to the next level. If you're struggling with your attitude today, add action steps and accountability, and go into the uncomfortable on a daily basis in order to change your attitude <u>and</u>
your life.

Chapter Summary

Slow down for just a moment and answer the following questions so that you may get the most out of this life changing book:

1. What was covered in detail in this chapter?

....

....

....

....

2. Of the topic, or different topics covered, which point was of most interest to you and why?

....

....

....

....

3. What is one action step you can take this week, that is relevant to this topic, that will propel you to create the life you desire?

....

....

....

....

Chapter 8
Standing In the Fire To Get Out of the Fire

Here's the greatest news you'll ever hear: you can accomplish almost any goal in life if you're willing to do the daily, necessary work and find someone to hold you accountable to do so. In other words, are you willing to do whatever it takes for as long as it takes to make your dream a reality? That's all you need to do.

Think positively? Heck yes. But don't get hung up on the law of attraction, vision boards or positive affirmations anymore. This book has given you a step-by-step process to follow in order to create the life you want. Follow it exactly as we've written it. As you have read in every chapter, many of the most successful authors and experts in the USA, support this philosophy, as well. This isn't something David Essel made up. This is something real, and you can give yourself the greatest gift by relaxing and following what all of these incredibly successful people have done. It's all in the action, baby!

As I look at my own life, I can tell you that the same principles apply in every aspect. I did not sculpt my body by thinking positively. I didn't create a rewarding career by visualizing it, and I didn't deepen my faith in God—or my spiritual practices—by creating a vision board of monks, chalices, and monasteries. It's the same for you. We've got to create a plan that includes daily action steps, regardless of our goals in life.

Once the daily work has become a habit, there's very little resistance remaining to achieve our goals. It's very much like making a new, more positive habit real in your life. Positive thinking is great, but the real goal is to get the conscious mind and the subconscious mind in alignment. When the conscious and subconscious minds are in alignment, we do what we know we need to do on a daily basis. Period. And the results are guaranteed. Whatever you want, within reason—remember I'll never be a starting guard for the Miami Heat—you can accomplish. It might take one year or three years or five years or maybe even longer for you to accomplish your goal, but it will be worth it!

I remember interviewing Nik Halik. He's the author of several books including, *The Thrillionaire*. He told me it took him 20 years to become financially free. He was a millionaire long before the 20 years were over, but at the end of 20 years of deep commitment to his multiple businesses, he now works one hour a day, seven days a week. And he does his work from anywhere. In his mid-40s, he can be on a trip to Iceland, where he loves to go, and still check in for his one hour a day meeting with his team members. He's created an incredible life doing whatever he wants, whenever he wants. For him money is never an issue, and neither is time. It took him 20 years to get there, but he is having the time of his life! That's what I want for you, as well.

Everyone says they want to be happy, successful, at peace, and to have excellent health. But are you personally doing whatever it takes, for as long as it takes on a daily basis to make this happen? Let's look at some final steps and stories to help you make your dreams come true.

⚓Self-acceptance can be an action step. When we talk about self-acceptance, we're talking about it in this present moment. Not when you get the body you want, but stripping down naked, standing in front of the mirror and accepting your body as it is right now. Then getting your clothes back on and getting your butt to the gym. Take 30 seconds right now. Put the book down, take all your clothes off and stand in front of the mirror, stare at your entire body, head to toe, and turn around. Get a mirror so you can see your backside, too. Take a moment and appreciate the fact if you have two legs, love them; if you have both arms, love them; whatever it is you have in this current moment, even if you weigh 800 pounds. Learn to accept where you are in life, and then grab the internal motivation to do what you need to do to change your body. Ask for help. Ask for help with all of your goals in life.

Coming into self-acceptance about our current financial situation is something we all need to do, as well. In other words, self-acceptance can be looked at as a form of gratitude. We're grateful for the money we have, even if it isn't what we want or even if it isn't enough. So we look at our bank statements, our savings accounts, the home mortgage, the rental properties, whatever we have, and we find a way to be grateful for this area of our life. And then go through every other area of our life and do the same thing. So many people think self-acceptance is a form of giving up, but nothing could be further from the truth. If you can learn to accept your body now, your financial situation, your relationship or lack of, you can start to prepare yourself for something much, much bigger and better. Don't settle for something that is not exceptional, but at the same time an action step for success would be to start to accept your body, relationships, and financial situation right now. Get to work. We all can do better at this.

Surrender to the reality of life. Too many times, through the use of positive thinking, affirmations, vision boards and even visualization, people try to escape the reality of life. They want to pretend that an obvious issue isn't there. "I'm not that overweight" or "I'm doing OK with my money", when they're swimming in debt. We do it to rationalize, justify, and deny the current reality so that we don't have to change!

This book is designed to awaken us out of denial. You must let go of judgment and justification if you want an exciting life, filled with pure abundance, financial independence, a rocking body, an incredible relationship and a heart open to love. You must leave behind rationalization if you want to forgive and be more compassionate. It's possible for anyone. And I'm going to prove it with this next story.

Scarlett Lewis is one of the most beautiful, compassionate, and forgiving people I have ever had the pleasure of speaking with. I've interviewed her several times on my national radio show and wanted so desperately for her to be a part of this book. Like Dianne Gray who you've read about earlier, Scarlett Lewis has faced the loss of a child, in one of the most horrific ways imaginable. She has used "surrender to the reality of what happened" as an action step to go out into this world and make a difference even after losing a young son.

The massacre at Sandy Hook Elementary School was being reported on national news. I was filled with the most incredible sense of loss, even though I didn't personally know anyone there. For Scarlett Lewis it was a different story. Her young son, Jesse, had left that morning for school, filled with a vibrancy of life. As Scarlett and her son, JT, would tell me during separate interviews on my radio show, young Jesse was filled with the spirit of joy. Everyone fed off of his infectious happiness. But this day would be different. Jesse would not return home. Here is Scarlett's story. She is so profoundly powerful, being able to come back from this tragedy while trying to make some sense out of it, and then using this horrific act to help heal the world.

SCARLETT LEWIS – THE WAY OUT IS THROUGH

"I have always been a 'glass half full' type of person. I believe this has helped my ability to alter my perspective in certain situations to have a more optimistic outlook. When my 6 year old son was murdered in his 1st grade classroom however, positivity was not going to be enough to get me through the trenches of shock, trauma and mourning. Especially when people around me were using positivity in order to avoid being present with me in my pain and to ease their own discomfort. "You had 6 years to love him!" "He is in a much better place!" "God wanted another angel!"

These seemingly supportive statements actually turned me off to positivity during my grieving. There was nothing good about having my son brutally murdered alongside 19 of his classmates, and six teachers and administrators in one of the worst school shootings in US history.

There was no way around the suffering for me. I was experiencing trauma and grief and soon learned that the two are separate and distinct. I was open to many different modalities of treatment and tried them all, from cranial sacral therapy, EMDR, MNRI, Brainspotting, Reiki, massage, hypnosis and traditional talk therapy. I practiced mindfulness, meditation and prayer. I learned that trauma can be treated and you can recover. Grief is a natural consequence of loss and I began to understand that dealing with it would be more of a process than a specific treatment. I learned to lean in to my emotions rather than avoid them and realized this would become a way of life, rather than recuperation. Thus by embracing the pain I uncovered a lot about myself, my limits, values and inner strengths.

The silver lining in tragedy is that it has inspired tremendous growth in me. It is through my journey of pain and suffering that I expanded and gained wisdom, found joy again and even discovered my mission in life! I had originally wanted to go around my grief, over, under, anything but walking directly through the fire.

But it was in the pilgrimage that I found salvation. Had I been able to escape or even fast forward through the extreme discomfort I wouldn't have cultivated the strength that feeds the resilience that allows me to utilize my experience to be instrumental in creating a world-wide movement to choose love.

I have learned that it is suffering that unites humanity, not the other way around. Everyone suffers to some degree. And interestingly, it is those who have suffered that have the courage to be present in my pain. It is through this authentic connection that hearts unite. If we could get from point a to point b without discomfort then there would be no impetus for growth. Progress and maturation come through tribulation thus the key is to embrace hardship, ask what lessons you can learn, and acknowledge this germination period as the process of blossoming!'

Compassion. Forgiveness. Grace. Inner peace. These things don't come to us by positive thinking or visualization, or vision boards. Scarlett explains quite beautifully that all of those things are the result of action steps into the uncomfortable on a daily basis. We truly need to awaken to the truth within her story and everyone's story in this book. You can have what you want but you're going to have to work for it. You're going to have to do things that you don't want to do. And when you do that—when you surrender to the reality of life—the end result can be stunning.

Surrendering to the reality of life leads us into becoming unstoppable. One of my best friends, Lee Witt, who wrote the book, *Become Unstoppable,* is a man of action. He's a man of deep spiritual beliefs. And he's a man of action. Did I mention that he's a man of action?

When I was traveling 40 weeks a year, I went out to Seattle every three months to speak to the followers of my national radio show. The very first time I went there, I was introduced one-on-one to "the man," Lee Witt. We had been in communication via email and phone before I arrived, as he was a rabid listener to our Saturday and Sunday three hour show. On this national show, we had the most powerful, positive guests every week, and Lee was one of the most positive thinkers I had ever met. After meeting in person, we became fast and deep friends. One day he called me to talk about progressing further in life than where he was right now.

"Lee you know you can do anything you set your mind to, but you're going to have to get uncomfortable and you know that. Meditation is a gateway to incredible success, at least that's what I found in my life. And because it's not in our wheelhouse—you and I are both action oriented in the physical world—we look at meditation as sitting and doing nothing. But it's really quite the opposite. When we sit and meditate, we open the internal world, so meditation is actually an action step. Try it. Let me help you. I know your life is going to change."

Lee doesn't do anything partway, and once he commits his life to a change, he makes the change 100%. His TV went into the closet never to come back out. His meditation session started to open up the potential from the inside out. From a position of public relations with one of the largest aerospace companies in the United States, Lee went on to create one of the most successful rock cover bands on the west coast of United States. He's written two books. He married the most unbelievable woman, and they sing together on stage on a regular basis. He's a profound motivational speaker.

Do you know how he accomplished all of this? Through powerful action steps: like meditation. He created space in the day to write after working 10 hours at a regular job. He created space in the day to rehearse with a seven piece band even after working a 60 hour work week. Follow Lee's path. We get out of life what we put into it. It's all about action. While Lee is one of the most positive thinkers that I've ever met, without profound action steps, his life would never have turned into the magical experience it has.

Becoming unstoppable also means doing what you'd rather not do, until it becomes a daily habit. My brother Terry, who I love very deeply, has a great story to prove the power of action steps to become more successful in business. He's an incredibly hard worker and an awesome positive thinker. But when you read the story, pay attention to what he did—it was uncomfortable—that created the success he's lived with for over 20 years.

TERRANCE ESSEL - PERSEVERANCE

"Twenty one years ago I started my business, Superior Fax Repair Co., on a "wing and a prayer" with virtually no start up capitol. I

did the usual, inexpensive business cards, a few mailings, a small ad in the yellow pages and listened to a lot of positive thinking cassette tapes. Yes, cassette tapes - it was 1994! After a few months, my brother David asked me how things were going. I answered truthfully "not very good, but I'm sure in time things will get better". He asked me what steps have I taken to promote my business? I said, business cards, yellow pages, a few mailers and a lot of "positive thinking" cassette tapes. He asked again, what steps have "you" taken? Hmm, well, not many actual "steps" I guess. He came up with a plan of me visiting 12 new companies each day for 60 days.

Believe me, every day I had to force myself to do this. I was scared and nervous. I didn't want to face rejection. Every day I'd pull up to another company, and sit and wonder how am I going to pull this off. I would say in the beginning, I might have had a 10% success rate, maybe one company a day would welcome me in their doors. It was really hard dealing with rejection after rejection. But then I saw a pattern. After about 30 days or so of doing it, I wasn't quite as nervous. After 60 days I was excited to get out there and show people what I can do to help them improve their business. After all I am a service oriented business, I believed in my product, and I believe I can help businesses run more effectively with our machines and our servicing of those machines.

It paid off. 6 months later I was averaging 3 billable calls per day! While the results weren't automatic by any means, I can honestly say that had I not followed David's "action step" plan, I would never have grown my business and certainly would not still be in business 21 years later. I wholeheartedly agree with David's premise that while positive thinking is a very important part of success, it alone will never build a dream or a business."

Believe in yourself! It's going to happen. But deal with your doubt. I don't care how positive a thinker you are—or how many powerful action steps you take on a daily basis—there's going to be periods of doubt, insecurity, and fear. And that's OK. Sometimes when we start to take serious action steps to create the life we want, the body, money or love relationship we want, we hit plateaus. We might see great success for a while, and then all of a sudden the weight is not coming off, we hit a financial drought, or our partner isn't responding like they were six months ago.

Anything can happen and probably will happen on your pathway to success. So what do you do about it? Well, as you probably can imagine, we have an action step for this, as well. When I hit periods of doubt with any of the above, I slow down. I find a pad of paper and pen, and begin to write all of the action steps that I'm taking in order to create the success I want. I write down where the advertising and marketing dollars are going, and everything else I need to be doing to make sure that I'm following my word and performing at my highest level possible. Have I gotten a little lazy in the last week or two? Am I still promoting our speaking and lecture series on a regular basis? Do the posts on social media need to be tweaked? Do the advertisements need to be changed slightly? Do the seminar titles need to be changed completely? Have I reached out to former clients to let them know of the new programs that we are offering that could benefit them, their friends or family? In other words, am I doing the work? Am I doing what's necessary to bring in the results that I'm looking for?

Then I write down the answer to each of these questions on paper. It doesn't take more than 15 or 20 minutes to find out if I'm putting the effort out there, or if I have gotten off track. You can use these same exercise if you've had a weight loss plateau, as well. You can write down, "Am I working out the same amount of minutes or hours per day? Am I putting the same effort in that I was 30, 60 or 90 days ago? Have I slacked off in any way? Have I hit a plateau; do I need to change my action steps in the gym? Do I need to do different cardio exercises? Do I need to change up my weight training routine? Do I need to be going to a yoga class to totally change everything, or if yoga is my deal do I need to get in the weight room to totally change everything and shatter the plateau my body has hit?' In other words, if you deeply evaluate on paper the area of life in which you were seeing great success—but you've currently reached a plateau—you can see the changes that need to be made pretty quickly.

The same thing can be applied to financial goals. Let's say someone had never saved very much before, and now they are starting to put money into savings, or the money market or mutual fund, stocks or investment properties. But for some reason they're starting to put less money in every month. Are they starting to spend emotionally again? Do they need to once again find ways to increase their income?

If the answer is yes, I'm doing everything I can, and I can prove it on paper to continue to grow the business, lose the weight or save the money, then I don't have to worry about being fearful, filled with doubt or insecurity. Life goes in cycles. I can accept that. This is just a down cycle, I'm doing everything I can, but I have hit a plateau. I don't need to have shame, guilt, fear, or doubt because I understand life isn't always on an upwards trajectory.

I can remember working with my business coach, Marleen Payne, a number of years ago, as I came to one of our weekly meetings filled with doubt. "I don't know what's going on. In the last 30 days I haven't made the money we projected. The eight months before, I nailed it every month, but I'm getting nervous. I'm not seeing the money coming in. And I don't see it coming in the next 30, 60 or 90 days, either. I'm not sure if I am doing something wrong, but I'm very anxious about my finances right now."

My coach listened to all of my fears and anxieties, and then she spoke. "David, I can tell you this without breaking confidentiality. I have another client, who is experiencing a similar situation. He's doing everything he can, but he's experiencing some setbacks, as well. He's very successful overall, as are you. So I just feel like we should take a big breath and ride this wave. The past eight months have been incredible in regards to your monthly income. You're doing great. You've continued with your daily and weekly action steps, and it has brought you this far. I think this is just a time to persevere. I'm really proud of you. Keep going strong."

Not only were her words reassuring and encouraging—but she was able to bring her experience of someone else that was going through the same thing at the same time, and "talk me down". Because while taking action steps are crucial, it's also crucial to give them time to work! One of the massive action steps everyone needs to take is to make sure that you're working with a coach, consultant or mentor that is right for you. It's not a sales pitch. It's pure reality. I was taught this years ago by my mentor Joe Cirulli, that having outside individuals and groups—like mastermind groups to hold us accountable—is a key step that all masters of success take. Get on the train. It's worth every penny you'll ever invest.

Another area in life where positive thinking alone won't get you very far is your sex life. Did you ever hear of anyone who positively thought their way to becoming a great lover? A great kisser? I don't think so! You've got to practice. Hey, this is where the book gets really fun.

I love my sex life. It's incredible. But I did not create it through the law of attraction, positive thinking, or vision boards. You can't put yourself on a vision board, and see yourself making love for hours. You actually have to practice the techniques that will allow you to connect at a deeper level. I was fortunate enough to have interviewed the top sex therapists in the USA, took courses and practiced what I wanted to become a reality in my sensual and sexual life.

One of the greatest teachers I've ever had in the world of sensuality and sexuality is the author, Dr. Barbara Keesling. By interviewing Barbara at least 10 times on my radio show, I was introduced to some brilliant sensual and sexual techniques right on national radio! Through her book, *How to Make Love all Night: And Drive a Woman Wild!* I learned the necessary techniques that all men can learn, to become an incredible and lasting partner. It's not rocket science. But it did take me about three months of practice—and that was fun, too—in order to master the art of being able to make love for as long as I wanted. I can just imagine all the women reading this book right now, racing out and getting Barbara's book for their boyfriends or husbands. But once again, it's the action steps that bring the end result, not fanciful thinking.

Another action step that a lot of people are uncomfortable with involve evaluating the people in your life right now, who you hang out with on a regular basis. In our coaching programs, I always advise my clients who want to make a lot more money, to make sure that in their sphere of influence, they have someone who's making much more money than they are today. I encourage them to go out and find friends who are incredibly successful financially. The same principle applies to any goal you have. If you're trying to lose weight, make sure that you are exposed to other people who are on the same path to eat correctly and exercise on a daily basis. Hang out with some people who are already in great shape.

Get humble. Get vulnerable. You can apply this to any other goal, too. If you want to deepen your faith? Make sure you're keeping company with deeply spiritual people. If you want to become more creative in life, the same thing goes. Make sure you have at least one highly creative person, a musician, an artist, or a designer in your life to learn from and be inspired by. If you want your marriage or relationship to go deeper, once again look around and make sure that you're not surrounded by people who are all struggling in their relationships.

You must stay away from gossipers in life! This is mandatory. People who gossip will hold you back quicker than anything. It's the same thing with victims. Have compassion for someone who complains all the time. Have compassion for someone who says the only reason they are in this financial situation is the government, or the only reason they struggle with weight is because of genetics, or the only reason they're unhappy is because of their partner. These are pure victims. And while you can have compassion for them, don't get sucked into their negativity. Similarly—if you're surrounded by people that are constantly saying they're going to do one thing, but rarely follow through—you're going to have to make some tough decisions there, too.

People with low levels of integrity, as well as, gossipers, and victims can demotivate you quickly. If you're hanging around with people who tell you they'll meet you for lunch at noon, and they show up at 12:30 or 12:45 and there's always an excuse, or maybe there's never an excuse that's just who they are—they're always late—accept it or move on. I know this sounds cruel, but I don't have time in life for people to become anchors in my existence. I'm not saying look for perfection, but you are the one who's in charge of who you keep company with, and it does have an influence over you, even if you don't realize it.

The same goes for what you watch, what you listen to, and what you read. If you want to become a huge success in life, with your mind, body, finances, and relationships, make sure that what you're listening to, watching and reading are in alignment with your goals. Stay away from reality TV shows. Fill your mind and your body with positive vibrations that come from radio, music, television, books, or magazines on the Internet where you have a greater selection. Be strong. Be bold. Don't follow the crowd. If people at work are talking about some drama on TV, walk away from it. If they are making jokes about other races, walk away from them.

Be powerful in your life. The more powerful you are through your actions in these areas I'm discussing right now, the more you will attract other powerful people. Now that's the law of attraction in action! That's the use of the powerful, positive side of the law of attraction. Walk away from people who do not serve you, and you don't have to do it in a negative way. Just start to spend less time with them. Be upfront with them. Let people know that you really don't have time for gossip, and that you'd rather talk about more fulfilling things like how to increase your income, how to lose weight and keep it off for good, how to deepen the love in your marriage, or how to make a bigger difference in this world.

Because our minds have been filled with the ridiculousness that's out there in the world of personal growth, things that drive me crazy like, "Think differently and become a millionaire, create the vision board of your perfect partner and attract your soul mate", it's going to take an all-out effort on your part to change your subconscious mind. Read this book over and over again, until it becomes a part of who you are. Until if I met you on the street, and I asked you what your favorite story was in chapter 4, you'd be able to tell me right off the top of your head. Of course, I'm smiling when I say this, but if you can get the stories and the principles in this book down, your life will be radically changed forever. I guarantee that. And so would any of the featured experts and writers in this book, as well.

Life is simply made up of one decision after another. Successful people understand this principle, and make sure every decision is based on reality. Know your goals. Today you can decide to start living life differently. Today you can make the call and start to bring more powerful people into your circle. Today you can decide to quit drinking or smoking, get to the gym, forgive someone who has hurt you, or to forgive yourself. Today you can decide to become a millionaire. It might take you 10 years, but you can make that decision today. I am with you every step of the way, in spirit if not physically. I want you to have everything you could possibly want in life. There are times I work with clients when I want their success more than they do—initially. But it's only a matter time.

If you continue to do the action steps into the uncomfortable, to go after your dreams, to do whatever it takes for as long as it takes, you will achieve your goals. I know you will. As I mention to individuals in our life coach certification course, I want them to be so successful that they can go out and impact thousands of people around the world. I want the same for you. Decide today that you're worth it. But remember, the only way you can prove you're worthy of getting anything new in life, is by taking the action steps that up until today you didn't want to take. Life is in your hands. Make the most of it. Invest time, money and effort into yourself daily.

If you have a hard time thinking of yourself, think of your children, do it for them, as well as yourself. Become the role model of incredible success, with a great body, great faith and great relationships. This is the legacy we can leave for generations to come. It's in your hands. Make the most of it. And once again, I'm with you every step of the way. Through this book, our courses, and just my mental energy, I am with you. Be powerful. That's what you're here to do. You're here to become the most complete you possible, the most successful you possible, the happiest you possible, and the most peaceful you possible. And it will only happen if you will live life differently than you've lived up to this very moment. Let's go!

Chapter Summary

Slow down for just a moment and answer the following questions so that you may get the most out of this life changing book:

1. What was covered in detail in this chapter?

....

....

....

....

2. Of the topic, or different topics covered, which point was of most interest to you and why?

....

....

....

....

3. What is one action step you can take this week, that is relevant to this topic, that will propel you to create the life you desire?

....

....

....

....

"Until you make the unconscious conscious,
it will direct your life, and you will call it fate."

– C.G. Jung

A Final Thought

Now is the time to become the limitless person you are meant to be. People who master the principles in this book will go on to create magic in their lives and the lives of those they love.

Your ability to master self-love, money, health, and love with another will become effortless as you put the principles of action into your life on a daily basis. All the hard work will pay off. You are limitless. But I say that not from a mental point of view only, you are limitless in your mind, body and spirit.

I remember a client that I worked with, who was trying to increase her income for years and years before coming into our program. Twelve months later, after mastering the power of daily action steps and unleashing her gorilla, during one of our sessions she said, "David, I just found out I have a health bill of $5000, and I'm not sure how I'm going to create that in just 48 hours." I told her that she had been doing everything in the world that she needed to in regards to action steps, and that this was her opportunity to have faith. Four hours later she called me up and excitedly left me a voice message saying that one of her clients had decided to purchase the largest personal growth package she offers at $5000!

I smiled as I listened to the message. The same thing can happen for you. Another client who worked with me for 16 sessions, to release her anger at her mother. Whenever they spoke on the phone or got together for family functions, it always ended up in an argument. They both had the desire to be right.

During our last session, she shared something magical that had happened. She decided that whenever she was getting close to a confrontation with her mother, she would interrupt her conversation with the statement, "Mama, I just want you to know I love you."

The first time she did it, her mother was taken aback. She didn't know what to say. They spoke a little longer and started to go down another path of disagreement. Within just a few seconds my client repeated the same statement, "Mama, I just want you know I love you."

The battle ended. She had mastered, through the writing exercises that she had worked with for 16 straight weeks, the release of resentments that she had held against her mother for over 40 years. She was experiencing life mastery. She saw how powerful she was and how powerful love was, when it came to her mother. In that moment, she became limitless. You can, too!

A really good question to ask right now is where does belief in ourselves come into play in all of this? What about those famous quotes. that center around the thought process. that if you believe in something strong enough you can achieve it? Is there any validity at all to these words?

Well, the short answer is of course, yes! There is validity in the notion that you must believe in something in order to achieve it. But my biggest concern with simple little quotations like this, is that the average person takes it upon themselves to say, "I just do not have enough belief in myself. I don't have the confidence. I don't have the self-esteem that other people do. If I was as confident as the people who have what I want, or if I had the breaks in life or the privileges that they've had, I could accomplish those things, too. But because I'm not like them, and I haven't been given a fair shake in life, it will probably never happen."

Many of us fall into the victim mindset from time to time in life. There are incredibly successful people in this world, that at one point thought that the only reason they didn't have what they really wanted was because of things outside of their control, such as the government, their partner, parents, their nationality or education. We can come up with all kinds of reasons why we don't have a strong belief in ourselves, but nothing will change until we look in the mirror and accept responsibility for ourselves from this point forward. This very fact is why positive thinking alone will never change our life, because we have to face ourselves, and that won't always be a warm and fuzzy positive experience. But the truth will set us free! We have to face the unknown and we have to let go of the past, which requires some kind of faith. Even if it is tentative. And having faith might mean that in spite of having negative thoughts something in you believes that things can change and that the way to do that will be shown to you.

The definition we will use for faith is: a belief in the yet unseen. I'm going to ask you to believe, starting right now with the power of your mind, that you can lose the weight you desire to lose, make the money you desire to make, attract the relationship you so want to experience, or save the current relationship you're in. I want you to believe that you can have what you don't have right now. But that belief or that faith, must be backed by your willingness to do the uncomfortable, to follow the steps that you would rather not do. Once you do this, your belief and faith in yourself will go through the roof. And I want that more for you than you may ever know.

So get out there right now! Don't waste another minute. Increase your belief in yourself and your goals by following the steps that we continue to repeat throughout this book. Create a written plan. Find someone to hold you accountable and watch your confidence grow.

Within the pages of this book we have shared stories of clients, celebrities, experts, and millionaires who created greatness in their life by doing exactly what we're asking you to do. Go back and read this book 10 more times. I'm being very serious right now. Your subconscious mind needs to be switched into the belief that you can have what you desire in life. But this will only happen when you follow a powerful action plan every day for the next 12 months.

When you master the principles in this book, you become 100% more positive in life. You expect great things to happen, and they do. Magic occurs. People will be drawn to your energy. Some may ask if you've lost weight, or if you found new love because somehow you've changed. And you have changed. You've achieved life mastery by doing the things that you didn't want to do, or that you didn't think would work. And now all of that effort, all of the hard work has paid off.

Welcome home. Welcome home to the limitless you. Welcome home to your true self.

INDEX FOR CONTRIBUTING AUTHORS

Cirulli, Joe
Joe Cirulli is the President of Gainesville Health and Fitness Centers, Gainesville, FL and one of the top entrepreneurs in the USA. From homeless to millionaire, Joe is an inspiration to millions.
www.GHFC.com

Collins, Dianne
Dianne Collins is the creator of the groundbreaking QuantumThink® system of thinking, 6-time award-winning bestselling author of "Do You QuantumThink? New Thinking That Will Rock Your World", popular media personality, and featured blogger on The Huffington Post.
www.diannecollins.com

Cyganiak, Tracie
Tracie Cyganiak is a business owner and amateur bikini competitor in the National Physique Committee. She loves spending time with family and inspiring others to achieve their fitness goals.
Email: tdance83@aol.com

Essel, Terrance
Terrance Essel is the CEO of Superior Fax & Laser and The Toner Kings Office Equipment sales and service / Toner sales in Syracuse, New York, and nationally. He has an awesome brother named David!
www.thetonerkings.com

Ford, Arielle
Arielle Ford is a gifted writer and the author of eight books including "Wabi Sabi Love: The Ancient Art of Finding Perfect Love in Imperfect Relationship"s and the international bestseller, "THE SOULMATE SECRET: Manifest The Love of Your Life With The Law of Attraction".
www.soulmatesecret.com

Gray, Dianne
Dianne Gray is President of Hospice and Healthcare Communications and Executive Director of the Elisabeth Kubler Ross Foundation, a beacon of hope for people and families facing the ultimate transition in life.
www.hhccommunications.com

Higdon, Ray
Ray Higdon is a two time bestselling author of "Vibrational Money Immersion". In just a few years Ray went from foreclosure, to building a multi-million dollar business. He now teaches people all over the world how to run profitable home businesses.
www.rayhigdon.com

Lewis, Scarlett
Scarlett Lewis is the founder of the Jesse Lewis Choose Love Foundation and is the mother of Jesse Lewis, one of the first grade victims at Sandy Hook Elementary. Scarlett wrote "Nurturing Healing Love", a book about her journey of hope and forgiveness.
www.jesselewischooselove.org

Pace, Natalie
Natalie Pace is the author of the Amazon bestsellers "The Gratitude Game, The ABCs of Money" and "You vs. Wall Street (aka Put Your Money Where Your Heart Is in hard cover). Natalie has been saving homes and nest eggs for 14 years, while at the same time earning the ranking of No. 1 stock picker.
www.nataliepace.com

Taylor, Eldon
Eldon Taylor is the New York Times bestselling author of "Choices and Illusions". He is a Fellow in the American Psychotherapy Association and a Certified Master Chaplain in the American Board for Homeland Security.
www.eldontaylor.com

Virgin, JJ
JJ Virgin is a Celebrity Health & Fitness Expert, New York Times Best Selling Author of "Sugar Impact Diet" and "The Virgin Diet".
www.jjvirgin.com

ABOUT DAVID ESSEL

David Essel, M.S. is the author of 9 books, a Master Life Coach and Teacher, Business, Relationship and Addiction Recovery Coach, International Speaker and Radio/TV Host. From athlete to poet, he has been labeled a "21st-century renaissance man" for his ability to inspire millions through the combination of his creative, authentic and philosophical energies and drive. David's professional presentations have drawn rave reviews from fortune 500 companies around the world. He is an avid tennis player, and spends every free moment at the beach.

DAVID ESSEL'S BOOKS

Angel On A Surfboard: Lessons About True Love From A Divine Messenger

Slow Down: The Fastest Way to Get Everything You Want (Hay House)

Heaven On Earth: God Speaks Through the Heart of a Young Monk

Rock Star: Finding God's Purpose for Your Life

The Power of Focus: How to Exceed Your Own Expectations in Life (e-book)

Phoenix Soul: One Man's Search for Love and Inner Peace

Language for the Heart and Soul: Powerful Writings on Life

The Real Life Adventures of Catherine "Cat" Calloway the 1st

David's books and CD's are available at www.amazon.com or for more info visit www.davidessel.com

3 WAYS TO GET INVOLVED WITH DAVID ESSEL

Why wait any longer? Work with David to create the life you want today… Take advantage of the teachings in this book to change your life now!

WORK WITH DAVID ONE-ON-ONE
Hire David today to help you create financial freedom, improve your health, save a relationship, find deep love, heal an addiction and/or change your attitude. As a Master Life Coach, all of David's one-on-one programs, have a one hundred percent money back guarantee.

"I am absolutely amazed at David's ability to help me grow in life! He has helped me in my business and love life. As a Medical Doctor, it has been hard to ask for help. David's expertise matches anyone I have ever met in life. I am empowered through his work. " ~Maureen Z., MD

BRING DAVID IN TO SPEAK TO YOUR AUDIENCE
As an inspirational speaker who has traveled all over the world, now is the time to bring David into your company to teach your associates the powerful techniques that he shares to help individuals and companies reach their highest potential.

"Our sales force, and employees are still quoting David. In an age of information overload, having such a lasting impact is truly impressive."
Misty Bryant, Nestlé

BECOME A CERTIFIED MASTER LIFE COACH
Be the change you want to see in this world, by working with David to become a Certified Master Life Coach. As one of the founding fathers in the life coaching industry, since 1996, he has helped thousands of people from around the world to become life

coaches, via phone, Skype or in person at one of his workshops.
For more information visit www.lifecoachuniverse.com

"David Essel is the top Life Coach in the USA."
The Image Workshop, Lifetime Television

For more information text our office today, 941.266.7676 or visit
www.DavidEssel.com right now.

⊙ the sun is ur instinct to shine from the center of ur life story. Above all else I want to _____.

☽ the moon is ur instinct to have a home. my mood always improves where _____.

☿ Mercury is ur instinct to communicate. I naturally communicate perspectives, a point of view about _____.

♀ Venus is ur instinct to love. I fall in love again & again when I _____.

♂ Mars is ur instinct to act. I always have energy to _____.

♃ Jupiter is ur instinct to philosophize, to sum it all up. I love exploring this area of my life because it gives me a larger perspective on things: _____.

♄ Saturn is ur instinct to commit. I want to mature over time in order to build _____.

⚷ Chiron is ur instinct to heal. I most want to be a healer in this area of my life: _____.

♆ Neptune is ur instinct to express soul. I most easily get out of my own way & allow inspiration to flow when I: _____.

♇ Pluto is ur instinct to express power. I want to understand & work w/ my own power around _____.

☋ The South Node of the moon is what
I have inherited from the past. When I
open my steamer trunk from the past I find:—

☊ The North Node of the moon is where
I am going, when I gaze at my future
& trust that I can become who I
always intended to be, I am becoming

♈ Aries explores will / to act
♉ Taurus stabilizes growth / to produce
♊ Gemini listens, perceives, communicates / to listen
♋ Cancer nourishes, cares, Incubates / to nourish
♌ Leo creates & celebrates / to celebrate
♍ Virgo explores the finest of function / to serve
♎ Libra loves beauty, balance, & fair play / to balance
♏ Scorpio knows through feeling / to transform
♐ Sagittarius unifies by making a map / to unify
♑ Capricorn supports standards of mastery / to teach
♒ Aquarius liberates by revealing the undeniable truth / to liberate
♓ Pisces encourages imagination / to let go

Made in the USA
San Bernardino, CA
02 May 2016